spin art

MASTERING THE CRAFT OF SPINNING TEXTURED YARN

jacey boggs

INTERWEAVE
interweave.com

EDITOR Ellen Wheat

ART DIRECTOR Liz Quan

COVER & INTERIOR DESIGN Lee Calderon & Julia Boyles

PHOTOGRAPHY Jeff Padrick

TECHNICAL PHOTOGRAPHY Ann Swanson

TECHNICAL EDITOR Maggie Casey

PRODUCTION Katherine Jackson

VIDEO STUDIO MANAGER Garrett Evans

VIDEO PRODUCER Rachel Link

CONTENT PRODUCER Rebecca Campbell

© 2011 Jacey Boggs
Photography © 2011 Interweave Press LLC
Illustrations © 2011 Kitten Adventure Boggs
Video © 2011 Interweave Press LLC

All fiber in this book was dyed, carded, and otherwise prepared by Mandie Chandler of Ewe Give Me the Knits.

Interweave Press LLC
201 East Fourth Street
Loveland, CO 80537-5655 USA
interweave.com

Printed in China by Asia Pacific Offset Ltd.

Cataloging-in-publication data not available
at time of printing.

ISBN 978-1-59668-362-4

10 9 8 7 6 5 4 3 2 1

*To Kitten: Without you my life would be
filled with far more "what ifs."*

*To Utah, Olive, and Zeke: Success comes
in many shapes; my biggest successes
are shaped just like the three of you.*

acknowledgments

Kitten, for the encouragement, the time, the editing, the illustrations, and the general super-awesomeness: you make me better. My kids, for their collective creativity and inspiration: you were the first things I made that I was proud of, and that has made all the difference. My mom, Sherris, for always being there to take up any slack. My pop, Brett, for loving handknits more than any non-knitter I know. You all are my family and made this book possible by making my life full and happy. I could write a much thicker book about how much I love you all.

Christie Brown, who swatched all the yarns in the book for me and who is a wonderful friend and travel companion (despite the snoring). Azur Zouiden, for never wavering.

Linda Ligon, who once told me that despite my outlaw appearance I had a beautiful aesthetic. Well, this outlaw thanks her for being a wonderful mentor and diligent cheerleader. Judith MacKenzie, for the inspiration, information, and constant support. Anne Merrow, my original editor, for the help, the guidance, the encouragement, the talks, and the wheel. I'd have been lst without her. Ellen Wheat, my new editor, who is so on top of things and thorough that it was hard for her to let that last sentence go to print without fixing it. She has been more than an editor— she has been an advocate and friend. Amy Clarke Moore, for teaching me the ropes. She is a kind and smart woman. Ann Swanson, for making me look and feel good. Her charm and generosity match her skill and creativity. Joaquin Phoenix mc, for being the face on the video monitor. He was a great fake-listener while I fake-taught him to fake-spin. Mandie Chandler, who took my extremely long and intimidating list of fiber types, preparations, and colors and delivered beyond my wildest imagination. She is a big part of the beauty on these pages. Maggie Casey, for the skillful technical editing: without her, people might think that I really don't know my maiden from my orifice. Beth Smith, my first and best long-distance fiber friend, for all the answers and advice. Gord Lendrum, for making a fantastic wheel and for using the word "fresh" instead of "interesting." Mark Brock-Cancellieri and Jonas Prida, who together with Kitten make up Save vs. Poison, without which I wouldn't know that spinning could be my job. Christopher and Joolee from Aminibigcircus: again, where would I be without you?

Also, thanks to: Interweave; Morgaine Wilder; Suzanne Pederson; Abby Franquemont; Garrett Evans; Diane Varney; Elizabeth Zimmerman; Jillian Moreno; Rebecca Campbell; Sarah Anderson; Lexi Boeger; Ravelry; Shuttles, Spindles, and Skeins; and all the spinners I've ever sat beside or across from. You all taught me so much.

contents

introduction

I learned to spin yarn barely two weeks after I learned to knit. Like so many new knitters, I was still knitting with craft store yarn, and when my internal calculations told me that to knit a sweater I'd be shelling out upward of $15, I was shocked!

I was naïve.

It was that naïveté that led me to think there must be a cheaper way, and so I purchased a used Louet S-10 online in the hope that I could spin my own yarn for cheaper than I could buy it. Like I said, naïve. Ten days later and $100 lighter, I sat down and put foot to treadle for the first time.

I was in love.

For the next two years, I spent at least four hours each day spinning in the corner of the dining room, behind the table, and in front of the window air-conditioning unit, while my son teethed, then crawled, then finally walked. I pored over every spinning and fiber book that my local library carried. When I'd absorbed all of

their information, I ordered from other libraries. I perused magazines. I scoured the Internet. If it was about spinning, I wanted to know it. My inchworm draw slowly changed to a comfortable short backward draft, then stretched to a graceful long draw. Plying came naturally, and the science of twist and balance seemed intuitive. Eventually I could spin without watching, and my yarns thinned and evened.

I spun and I knit and I was happy. I also blogged. Handspun yarn was not easily found online at that point, so when I started posting process and finished pictures, readers started asking to buy. The most daring thing I spun and sold was singles, but mostly traditional 2-plies paid the bills.

And then the experiments began.

Some artistic spinners were pulling some fun textural stunts, and I tried my hand at them. After having spent so many hours working to make my yarns even and balanced, though, the lack of control and durability in

these textured yarns frustrated me. Still, I set about learning everything I could about the tricks and techniques that these less traditional spinners were doing or had done in the past. Then I experimented with how to adapt and develop what I'd learned in order to create more controlled and sturdier yarns. I realized these two aspects, controlled spinning and creative textural techniques, could and should be married. All of the following skills directly influenced my textural spinning and made it better:

having control over one's hands and feet; understanding different types of fibers; knowing how twist works, where it accumulates, and how it impacts plying; and how staple length affects drafting, hand distance, and drape. Knowing how to spin is paramount. My controlling nature finally paid off in demanding that everything be exact, neat, and durable. I scaled things down, refined hand movements, and introduced anchors. After I'd adapted what was already out there, I started experimenting with new textures and combinations.

And the world opened up.

Today, I teach workshops all over the world. I teach the textural techniques in this book—the hand movements for them, the reasons and science behind them, what works and what doesn't work, and why. But what I really hope that the spinners I teach take away with them is that the more you learn about spinning, the better spinner you'll be. That the old adage, "Know the rules before you break them," doesn't really apply. You can't break the rules of fiber and spinning and still produce a good yarn: you have to learn the rules well enough that you can work inside their parameters to get the fiber to produce the yarn you want. Traditional spinners will gain insight, dexterity, and control when they venture to spin texturally. Textural spinners will gain insight, dexterity, and control when they endeavor to spin traditionally. Traditional and textural spinning are two sides of the same coin—two plies in the same yarn. One just happens to be bumpier than the other.

equipment & supplies

Spinning textured yarns should not take more or fancier equipment than spinning traditional yarns does. It is all yarn, and if you have the hand and fiber control that every spinner tries to develop, then what can be done big can be done small, what can be done haphazardly can be done with control, and what can be done accidentally can be done intentionally. There is no reason to buy a bulky wheel with a huge orifice and slow ratios if you don't want to. You should (and can) use the wheel you use every day for everything in this book (except extreme tailspinning). In fact, there are only a few special considerations for wheels with regard to spinning textured yarns.

orifices

There are currently several types of orifices on the market—traditional flush innies, outies, deltas, and O-rings. Any type of orifice will work with almost all of the techniques in this book. For the very few that are ill-matched for particular orifices, alternative methods are given.

As for orifice size, every yarn in this book (except one, extreme tailspinning) was spun with a Lendrum DT with a standard head and a 7/16-inch orifice. That is an average-sized orifice, and there are very few wheels out there that come standard with something smaller. Unless you are planning to insert huge, hard, foreign objects into your yarn, the orifice you have should do just fine. If you do plan to make giant yarns, a lot of wheels can be fitted with bulky flyers, but you don't need them to create beautiful, striking, textured yarns.

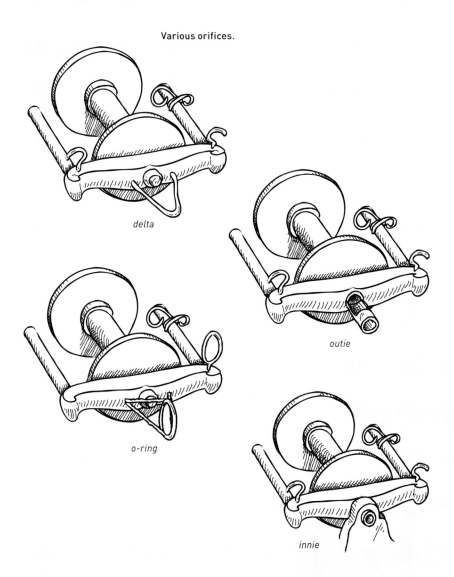

Various orifices.

delta

outie

o-ring

innie

guides

Once the yarn enters the orifice, it is fed onto the bobbin through guides, which may be hooks, sliders, or automatic sliders. You can spin all the techniques in this book with any type of guide, though there are those that make it a bit easier.

The easiest, least troublesome guide for textural yarns is the slider. Since it is a smooth circle, no matter the texture of the yarn, as long as it is not bigger than the guide it will slide right through. Automatic sliders (such as WooLee Winders) are lovely to spin with, and once you get accustomed to the techniques, they can be used effortlessly for these yarns as well.

But in the beginning, with all the starting and stopping that takes place in the learning process, they can be a hindrance.

Because of the texture of some of the yarns, hooks are the most difficult guides. Anything loose or too puffy has a tendency to get snagged on them, which causes more stop and start than you would be doing otherwise. There are a few things you can do to resolve this problem. The best, and perhaps the most difficult in the beginning, is to make sure that you are spinning your yarns with the correct amount of twist—not too loose or with too many loose ends. This is true for

all of the techniques with the exception of tailspinning, where the structure of the intact locks is just too much to evade snags on standard guide hooks. Another thing that helps is to turn all the hooks inward, except for the first one and the one you are currently spinning onto, which minimizes the number of hooks your yarn can get snagged on. Another popular solution is to replace one side of your flyer hooks with L-shaped shoulder hooks available at any hardware store for less than a fancy cup of coffee. Finally, there are sliders you can purchase that fit about any wheel. They are a joy to work with, and make spinning textured yarns much easier and faster.

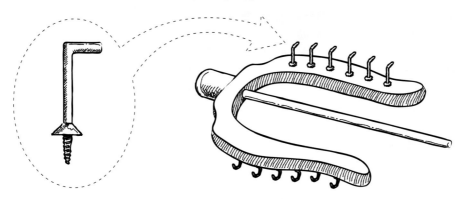

Installing L-shaped flyer hooks.

tensioning devices

There are three main types of tensioning devices on spinning wheels: double drive, scotch tension, and irish (or bobbin-led) tension. All three work for any of the techniques in this book, but irish tension can require a bit more adjusting for textured yarns. Sometimes these techniques require less tension (pull-in) than irish tension is able to provide. Two remedies work well in this situation. First, don't be afraid to take the brake band off completely. If that doesn't decrease the tension enough and your wheel has hooks as guides, lace the yarn back and forth between the guides.

This practice is used commonly with lace spinning and works just as well for some of the textured techniques where you don't want to have to fight the pull-in of the wheel while your hands are trying to accomplish new or complicated movements.

Lacing for decreased tension.

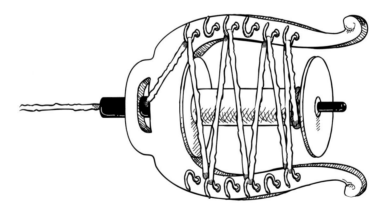

tips for spinning textured yarns

Read these tips Be sure to read this tips section first and often while reading and working from this book. The tips will help in the beginning, and as you get better at the techniques, they will make more and more sense.

Know how best to use this book This book is intended to be read and worked from front to back and then further employed as a reference book. The techniques are presented in two sections: Singles Techniques and Plied Techniques. For the most part, the earlier techniques require less finger dexterity and develop new skills or mindsets. The later techniques build on the earlier ones.

Get good with ratios Experiment with the different ratios available to you. Remember it is like a geared bike— the bigger your pulley, the slower your flyer or bobbin turns, causing less twist to enter the yarn; and the smaller the pulley, the faster the flyer or bobbin turns, causing more twist to enter the yarn. Bigger pulley—less twist, good for thicker yarns. Smaller pulley—more twist, good for thinner yarns.

Learn to manipulate tension When you increase the tension by tightening your brake band (in scotch tension), or both bands (in double drive), your yarn will pull in quicker and with more gusto, thereby zipping into the orifice before gathering much twist. When you decrease the tension on your wheel, your yarn will pull in slower and with less enthusiasm, thereby sticking around outside the orifice longer and gathering more twist.

Note: Check the "Tips for Technique" for each skill: Many of the techniques in the book refer you to a "tip" or two elsewhere in the book. Before you attempt a spinning technique, turn to the referenced pages and learn from the tips to master the skills.

Don't get frustrated Spinners often feel that since they know how to spin, these new techniques should come naturally, even easily. This is generally not the case. Give yourself a break—realize your hands are learning new movements and skills. It will take them, and you, a while to get the hang of it.

Use commercially spun yarns (it's okay!) Even if you plan to spin your own laceweight eventually, consider starting with a commercial yarn to minimize waste of fiber and time. Do not use thread. If it doesn't break while you're spinning it, it will when it gets worked up.

Match your commercially spun yarn to your fiber When I use commercial laceweight in my handspun yarns, I try to match it to the yarn I am spinning, both in color and fiber content. I find that if the two strands have similar fiber content, I can better predict how the finished yarn is going to act in different situations, temperatures, and washing circumstances.

Introduce twist into commercially spun yarn for better balance If you are using commercially spun yarn as a structural element in your handspun (for plying or as a core), you will improve the overall balance of your finished yarn if you introduce some extra twist into your balanced commercial yarn. All you have to do is run it through your wheel in the opposite direction that you will be spinning it for the technique. Your goal, when you incorporate this commercial yarn, is to spin it in the opposite direction of the twist you added so that the commercially spun yarn ends up back at its original balance point.

Put lazy kate in her place Your lazy kate should be at your feet and on a parallel plane with your hands as they are working. This way your yarn pulls straight up, rather than at an angle, which can give you unpredictable tension.

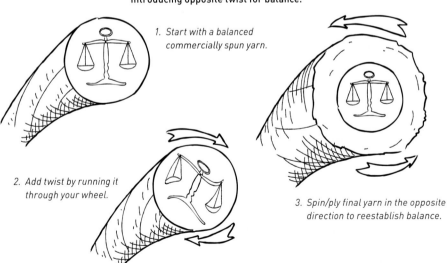

Introducing opposite twist for balance.

1. *Start with a balanced commercially spun yarn.*

2. *Add twist by running it through your wheel.*

3. *Spin/ply final yarn in the opposite direction to reestablish balance.*

Spin the first few and last few yards evenly For those intending to use the yarn for knitting, to ease casting on and binding off, spin a few even yards about the average thickness of the yarn you plan to spin at both the beginning and end of a yarn.

Slow down while you are learning While it is possible to spin textured yarns at high ratios and with a quick step, I recommend slowing way down until you get the hang of a technique. Don't be afraid to stop treadling while your fingers catch up with your feet. Remember, your feet know what they are doing, but in many cases, your hands are learning new skills.

Spin closer to the orifice In textured yarn spinning, your hands should be a bit closer together and closer to the orifice than in traditional spinning, especially when first learning the techniques.

Try it my way first Every spinner spins uniquely. Exactly how you hold and use your hands is distinctive to you. The instructions in this book do not aim to change the way you spin, just to teach you new techniques. If, however, you have never spun a technique before, try it my way first so that you understand what the goal is and then adapt it to your own personal spinning style.

Don't make your hands switch jobs In my experience teaching, I have found that spinners are about evenly split when it comes to which hand is in front and which hand is in back. So please don't feel prompted to change your dominant hand to match mine. This book doesn't refer to right and left hands, but to front or drafting hand and back or fiber-supply hand. This way, you can let your hands do the jobs they are used to doing while they are learning these new skills.

Give your bobbin-led wheel de-tension If you are using a bobbin-led wheel (irish tension) and feel like you are fighting to keep your yarn from winding on the bobbin, try taking your brake band all the way off or lacing the yarn between the hooks.

Take the time to anchor Master the anchors of different techniques. There is nothing more frustrating than spending lots of time trying to create a feature in a yarn only to have it fall out or slide around because it is not anchored properly.

Finish your yarns right Take the time to master the dexterity and control needed to make a sturdy textured yarn, and it won't require special finishing. A textural yarn can be finished in exactly the same way a traditional yarn is finished: a warm or hot bath or steam, a gentle snap (or a vigorous snap, or no snap at all if that is your preference), then hanging, untensioned and unweighted, to dry.

Never weight or tension-set your knitting yarns Textural yarns are not different from traditional yarns. If you wet, stretch/weight them, and let them dry, you relieve them of elasticity, loft, and life. You will also give them a false balance that will disappear as soon as the yarn gets wet again.

part one

SINGLES
TECHNIQUES

wraps

Wraps are just that—strands and threads that wrap around the yarn you are currently spinning. Wraps are one of the easiest ways to add a bit of interest to a traditional yarn. They take little dexterity and few supplies and can have an enormous impact on the look and feel of a yarn. Wraps do not have to be center stage; they are good at humbly being a simple layer in a more complex yarn. You will see examples of and instructions for this in later chapters.

A wrapped yarn is a singles with two or more layers. The first layer is the fiber that becomes the actual yarn: generally any fiber and fiber preparation will work. The second layer is the wrap and is only limited by your imagination. Each technique, however, has different tensile-strength needs depending on whether the wrap is structural or aesthetic, so keep this in mind when choosing. A good rule of thumb is if the wrap uses roughly the same amount of yardage as the final yarn, then it is structural and should be of sound

material. But if the wrap uses quite a bit more yardage than the final yarn, then it is decorative, and it is okay to use things with less strength, such as Lurex, metallic thread, or sewing thread. This general rule will keep your wraps unbroken and your yarns strong.

A short forward or short backward draw is the easiest to use when spinning a wrapped yarn. However, for the more adventurous, autowrapping and tornado can be combined with corespinning, and a long draw has been known to make a great autowrapped woolen yarn.

If you have spun mostly traditional yarns up to this point, wraps are a good and not-too-overwhelming place to start your textural yarn journey. In this section, you will learn the racing stripe, which can be used later for affixing small foreign objects; the autowrap, which is so automatic it almost doesn't need you there at all; and the tornado, which will blow you away with its exuberance.

techniques in this chapter | racing stripe • autowrap • tornado

racing stripe

Racing stripes, also called barber poles or carry-alongs, are the quickest and easiest wrap in town. They are essentially a singles yarn with two plies: you can mix and match your fibers and strands for endless variety. But don't let its simplicity fool you. This wrap can be a workhorse for more elaborate textured yarn techniques.

fiber

The base of this yarn is a singles, and any fiber and fiber prep will work. The racing stripe can be commercially spun or handspun (anything from laceweight to novelty yarn). This is a case of your yarn is only as strong as your weakest strand. If your finished yarn gets pulled or yanked, a weak racing stripe will break, so you want to avoid simple sewing thread and use something with a bit more strength.

Prepare your fiber however you like and arrange your racing stripe ball (bobbin, spool, or cone) at your feet on your front/drafting-hand side.

wheel setup

This technique does not dictate the setup of your wheel, so set it up for the singles that you will be spinning. If you are going bulky, set it up slow (on a big pulley) with high uptake: if you are going thin, go faster (smaller pulley) with less uptake. If you are using a commercially spun racing stripe, you can spin in either direction, but if you're using a handspun racing stripe, spin in the opposite direction of your racing stripe.

The sample yarn is a base singles of Polwarth combed top (Z-spun) and a racing stripe of Merino and silk handspun (S-spun).

spinning

Spinning a worsted singles using a short backward draw while wrapping it with a prespun yarn sounds tougher than it is. Really, the only trick to spinning with racing stripes is not to overthink it.

Join the fiber to the leader and while holding the racing stripe loosely across the palm of your front/drafting hand, start spinning by pinching the fiber in your front/drafting hand and pulling your back/fiber-supply hand backward **(STEP 1)**. Then follow the twist with your front/drafting hand **(STEP 2)**. That's it. Just spin the yarn and let the racing stripe wrap around it **(STEP 3)**.

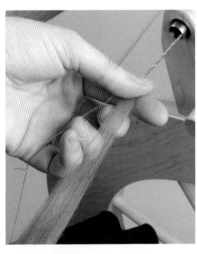

autowrap

Autowrap—the name says it all. With a traditional orifice, this is a wrap that wraps itself automatically. If you have an outie orifice, a delta, or a ring, you can get similar results, but it's not quite so automatic. Unlike the racing stripe, an autowrap wraps irregularly and with a different twist angle than the underlying singles. Requiring minimal labor, this great technique gives a yarn mystery and zing with its peculiar perpendicular wrapping and just gets more impressive when combined with other techniques, as you'll see in later chapters.

TIPS FOR TECHNIQUE: racing stripe (see page 22).

fiber

Like all the wraps, any fiber or prep will work for the base yarn. However, this technique is one of the few where an element of the yarn (the wrap, in this case) doesn't require much tensile strength. Since the wrapping strand is more than triple the length of the base singles, there is no reasonable chance of it being stretched taut. So go ahead and grab those spools of shiny or metallic thread, Lurex, or novelties. They work and look great.

Place the autowrap strand on either side at your feet and as even with the orifice as possible. The slightest bit of tension can cause the autowrap strand to pull tight and, instead of wrapping, to disappear inside the yarn as it is being spun. If you are using handspun for the autowrap, you may find that the bobbin's weight produces too much tension. If this happens, just wind it off into a ball and pop the ball in a bowl at your feet.

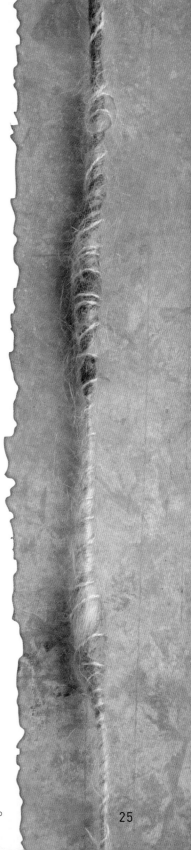

wheel setup

This technique does not dictate the set-up of your wheel. Set up the wheel for the singles you will be spinning. If you are using a commercially spun wrap, you can spin in either direction, but if you are using a handspun wrap, spin in the opposite direction of the wrap.

The sample yarn is spun Z, has a core spun from a textured, carded batt, and an autowrap of brushed mohair.

spinning

If you have what I call an innie orifice, one that is flush or almost flush with your maiden, this wrap is a breeze. Simply start spinning the singles and the autowrap together with a short forward or short backward draw, as if you are spinning a racing stripe **(STEP 1)**, then drop the racing stripe, and it becomes the autowrap **(STEP 2)**. That's right, just drop it and keep spinning. The autowrap will automatically wrap around the singles, creating an irregular wrap that adds a bit of mystery and intrigue to your yarn. Don't worry if the autowrap disappears into the orifice. That is exactly what is supposed to happen.

Remember to let your yarn run into your orifice at a regular pace and in short-ish intervals. If you attempt a modified long draw or even allow the singles you are spinning to get too long before you let it enter the orifice, you will end up with long sections where the autowrap is not accumulating much twist and therefore is spun alongside the core rather than wrapping around it.

If you have a delta, ring, or an orifice that extends beyond the maiden, and you try to do an autowrap in the above-described manner, you will likely spend a great deal of time unwrapping yards and yards of autowrap that automatically wrapped around the outie orifice, delta, or ring. There is a solution, but it takes a finger, some patience, and a bit more dexterity.

Everything is set up the same way, but when you're ready to release the racing stripe and start autowrapping, extend one of the fingers of your back/supply hand—I usually use my pinkie—and use it to guide the autowrap **(STEP 3)**. You don't have to do too much; just keep the wrap from traveling into the orifice. This isn't the most comfortable position, and doing it for extended periods can cause cramping, so use caution.

Autowraps of different materials will not only give you different looks but will wrap differently as well. Some will create big, loose loops, while others will wrap tighter or with crinkles or folds. So experiment.

tornado

The tornado is the most dramatic wrap. Fiber artist Lexi Boeger introduced me to this technique: three or more strands wrapped irregularly and loopily around a handspun singles. Varying greatly depending on the materials used, yarns incorporating the tornado technique range from merely exciting to truly electrifying.

TIPS FOR TECHNIQUE: racing stripe (see page 22).

fiber

Any fiber can be used to spin the core of a tornado yarn, but it should be something loosely prepared. I'm not normally one for splitting and predrafting fiber out to the diameter you are going to spin, but this is one technique that is made much easier by extreme splitting and predrafting. For the tornado wraps, choose at least three different wraps. Like the autowrap, since the yardage of your wraps far exceeds the yardage of your handspun singles, they are very unlikely to be pulled to their breaking point, so you don't need to consider

tensile strength. Grab anything that strikes your fancy, including threads, metallic threads, Lurex, novelty yarns, brushed mohair, or handspun. Experiment with the types of strands you use to tornado. Mixing different weights, textures, and drapes gives wonderful and unexpected results.

Place all the strands at your feet on your fiber-supply/back hand. There should be a bit of space between the strands to ensure they can all be pulled freely without too much tension or tangling.

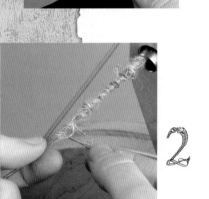

wheel setup

This is one of the slower, more fiddly techniques, so set up your wheel on one of its slowest (biggest) pulleys. You don't want the uptake pulling too much, so set the tension to medium-light and increase as needed. You can spin this yarn in either direction, but if you are using handspun as your tornado strands, spin in the opposite direction of the handspun singles.

The sample yarn's core is a Bluefaced Leicester combed top base, and the tornado strands are handspun Merino and silk (S), Polwarth (S), thread, and commercial brushed mohair and silk. The tornado is spun Z.

spinning

Start spinning the fiber as a singles using the tornado strands as racing stripes. When you are ready to begin the tornado, slow down your treadling and hold the tornado strands out from the fiber at somewhere between a 70- and 90-degree angle **(STEP 1)**.

Since the fiber is stripped and predrafted, you don't have to deal much with it except for using your front/drafting hand to let the twist travel slowly down while you use your other hand to wrap the wrapping strands in a kind of shuffling motion **(STEPS 2 AND 3)**.

This technique relies on twist, so you do have to keep treadling, but at least in the beginning, treadle as slowly as you can while still keeping your wheel going. You want enough twist to make a strong, stable singles yarn because that is where all your yarn structure comes from; but you don't want so much twist that your singles is grossly overspun, or your tornado looks like a bundled corespun yarn. The tornado is slow going in the beginning, and even after you master it, it is still much slower than most textural yarn techniques. The drama of the yarn, however, is worth the plodding spin.

corespinning

Corespinning is a gateway technique. It can be as subtle as the materials and the hand you use to make it, so it is great if you are on the fence about getting too arty with your yarn. On the other hand, with more flamboyant materials, it can produce one of the wildest yarns around. This technique can produce dizzyingly diverse yarns, each made unique by the kind and amount of fiber used, the treadle speed, and the core diameter. It uses neither a short nor long draw, but because of the fiber prep and the mechanics of the technique, corespun yarns generally have more in common with woolen yarns than worsted yarns: they tend to be lofty, light, and airy. Corespinning is also a fantastic way to stretch a prized fiber and create a singular, highly usable yarn.

A corespun yarn consists of two layers: the inner prespun core and the outer fiber that wraps around the core on an almost perpendicular plane. There are no rules prescribing what these two layers should be made of, which means your yarn can have an almost unending array of looks.

The first technique covers basic corespinning. You will learn how to pick out and prepare your supplies, as well as the mechanics of the technique. Basic corespinning alone could keep you spinning enough to tire your treadling legs and exhaust your fiber stash; but don't miss out on cocoons and the black sheep of the corespinning family—the ever-wild tailspin and extreme tailspin. All use subtle variations on the same basic hand mechanics to produce vastly different yarns.

techniques in this chapter | basic corespinning • cocoons • tailspinning • extreme tailspinning

basic corespinning

Basic corespinning is anything but basic. This section will show you how to spin a balanced corespun yarn, how to choose and adjust a core, what fiber works best, and exactly how to move your hands so that your fibers lie perpendicular-esque instead of the more traditional parallel-ish.

TIPS FOR TECHNIQUE: introducing twist into commercially spun yarn for better balance (see page 16).

fiber

Core The core is the strength of a corespun yarn, so make sure your core has integrity and good tensile strength. Stay away from thread or yarns that break easily. Also, unless you decide to use it as a design element, the core will not be visible, so don't worry about its aesthetic. In fact, it is a good way to use up yarn that you don't particularly like. Handspun or commercial, laceweight, bulky, and anything in between will work. Since you will be wrapping a very thin layer of fibers around the core, select a core that is a bit thinner than you want your final yarn to be. If you are aiming to create a thin yarn, use laceweight; if you want something bulkier, break out the worsted or bulky yarns.

Because you are wrapping fiber around a core, the wrapping fiber is being bundled down onto the core rather than accumulating twist in the traditional way. The core, however, is accumulating every treadle of twist.

This presents an unusual issue regarding balance. Corespun yarns are most commonly left as singles, because attempts to balance the twist by plying tend to balance the core while unwrapping the fibers you just corespun around it. Take a moment and read about introducing opposite twist into commercially spun yarns in the Tips section (see page 16). If you decide to handspin a 2-ply core for the corespun, overply it so that when you corespin in the opposite direction, you will end up with a balanced 2-ply core. Alternatively, you can spin two singles and ply them together as you corespin, resulting in a balanced 2-ply core and a supple drape.

Instead of a 2-ply core, you also have the slightly less time-consuming option of using a handspun singles yarn. Keep in mind, though, that cutting this corner will leave you with a yarn that can't be perfectly balanced because you can't spin a singles yarn and then corespin in the opposite direction. If you were to do that, you would end up with unspun—and therefore unstable—fibers as the core. Singles will also be weaker and less stable than plied yarns. If you decide to go the singles-for-a-core route, spin a worsted singles with very little twist, then corespin it in the same direction as the single twist. This adds more twist and delivers a core that is a solid singles. This will not make a balanced yarn, but it can make a very sturdy one. And if you are careful not to overdo the twist, it shouldn't bias when used in a knit stitch.

Outer Wrapping Fiber Now for the fun part: What fiber do you want to corespin? Although almost any fiber can be corespun, some fibers work better and are easier than others. All, however, will produce interesting results. Roving, rolags, and carded batts all use the same basic hand mechanics and can yield similar yarns. The exception is combed fiber or top. Because of the perfect alignment of combed fibers, you will tend to lose a bit of the wooliness that makes a corespun yarn special. It is also a bit less forgiving than carded fibers, so when you are first starting out, it is best to use carded fiber.

While commercial roving, rolags, and well-carded, smooth batts work well, multifibered carded batts are really where corespinning kicks off its shoes and comes alive. Spinning a breathtaking yarn from these batts can be challenging at times, but corespinning is a fitting approach. It stretches those precious batts into more and bulkier yardage, because none of those fibers gets lost making up the center of the yarn. On top of that, it nicely showcases their uniqueness and beauty.

Once you've chosen, strip the fiber out into chunks that you can easily hold in your back/fiber-supply hand. Place the core at your feet on your front/drafting-hand side.

wheel setup

Since, with corespinning, you are not adding twist to the fiber but to the already spun core, it is best to set up your wheel on a big pulley for minimum twist accumulation. Uptake should be low to moderate—you don't want it pulling against you, but you want it to pull in when you relax your hold on the yarn. You can spin in either direction, but I find that the mechanics of corespinning work best if the fiber wraps over the top of the core.

The sample yarn has a commercially spun 2-ply core with added S-twist, and the wrapping fiber is a medium-textured carded batt. It was corespun in the Z direction.

spinning

Two common problems that crop up in corespinning are lack of twist control (the yarn ends up overspun) and lack of fiber control (the spinner lacks control over the diameter of the final yarn). These occur because we're traditionally taught to hold the core with one hand and the fiber with the other and to hope that when we touch the two together, they will catch and create a yarn. If you've tried this, you've probably experienced some of the frustration that comes with not having enough (or if you're like me, not having total) control over your spinning. The solution to this problem is easy and already in your hands. In fact, it is part of your hand: your thumb and index finger.

Start treadling slowly. Remember that all the twist is going into the core, and the only effect it has on the wrapping fibers is to bundle them down tighter and tighter. For a stable, long-lasting yarn, don't let the corespun fiber float about the core. For a balanced yarn with good hand, don't bundle it down too hard and tight. Also, if

you introduce too much twist, you risk diminishing, even eliminating altogether, the characteristic loftiness of a corespun yarn. The tighter you spin this yarn, the less you feature the perpendicular fibers and the less air you leave in it, making it less lofty and warm.

For the first few inches, spin the core and fiber together as a singles yarn. This situates it and gives you something secure to tie off to when you are done. Make sure your hands are not too far from the orifice and are close to each other. The core should be held across the palm of your front/drafting hand; the fiber mass should be in your fiber-supply/back hand, pulled to the side at something akin to a 90-degree angle **(STEP 1)**.

Using the thumb and index finger of your core-holding hand, pinch a small amount of fiber from the fiber mass and slowly pull the fiber mass away from the core **(STEP 2)**. You don't want much fiber stretched between your two hands—the amount dictates the

3

diameter of your finished yarn. If you want thicker yarn, use a thicker core instead of more fiber (adding fiber yields a poofier yarn, as well as adding bulk). Pull your hands apart just a bit less than the average staple length of the fiber you are spinning. Don't let a thin layer here worry you: you'll feel it start to give before it separates from the mass. Now, loosen your grip on the core by opening your thumb and index finger (STEP 3) and bring your fiber-supply hand close to the core again (STEP 4). While you are bringing these hands close together, slide your core-holding hand toward your body, along the length of the core, so that the fiber covers a section of the core instead of building up in one spot. This helps ensure that the fiber covers the core in an even-ish layer.

Now that you're back at the starting point with your hands close together, it's time to pinch fiber off of the mass with your thumb and index finger again. Pull the fiber mass away from the core and keep going. Look at you: you're corespinning!

4

cocoons

Cocoons, surprising little cocoon-shaped bundles of fiber spun into a singles yarn, are great fun to spin and knit. They are a bit easier to spin if you first try your hand at corespinning, since cocoons are short sections of corespinning with top and bottom anchors added.

TIPS FOR TECHNIQUE: basic corespinning (see page 34).

fiber

Any fiber or fiber prep will work for the base yarn, keeping in mind, of course, that this is going to stay a singles yarn. The choices for cocoon fiber are innumerable: protein fiber, cellulose, man-made, sparkle, threads, and the list goes on. They all work and give great results.

wheel setup

Since this yarn is a singles, it doesn't need much twist. While you would usually handle this with a medium- big pulley and a firm uptake, cocoon construction is hindered by strong uptake, so it is necessary to choose a bigger pulley and slow down the treadling a bit. Set the uptake slightly lower than medium so that while your hands are building anchors and cocoons, you don't also have to keep the yarn from disappearing into the orifice. Don't, however, set the uptake so low that it doesn't pull in when you release your hand tension. This yarn can be spun in either direction.

The sample yarn is a Merino and silk fiber singles with Merino and silk cocoons, spun in the Z direction.

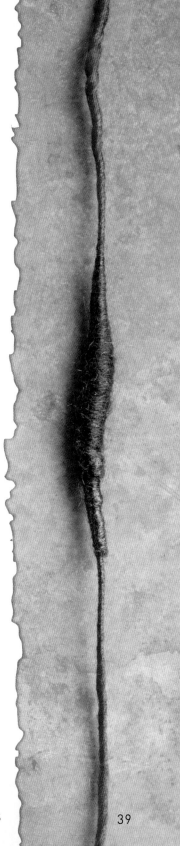

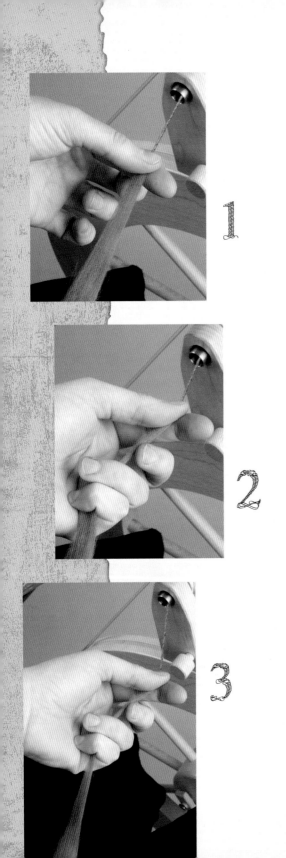

1

2

3

spinning

To begin, spin a yard or two of your singles using a short backward or forward draw and make sure you are happy with the thickness and amount of twist. Once you settle on a yarn thickness, grab a small chunk of your contrasting cocoon fiber.

Predrafting under the cocoon The real trick to this technique lies in a basic spinning mechanic: twist accumulates in thin spots. This rule is an important one to remember when spinning a bundle of fiber over the top of a base yarn. If you spin a cocoon over a thick spot in the yarn, nothing holds it in, nothing bundles or anchors it down. If you spin a cocoon over a thinner spot, the twist accumulates there and holds the cocoon in place. So, you must make sure that the portion of the singles over which you spin the cocoon fiber is slightly thinner than the yarn surrounding it. A small amount of predrafting and testing makes this fairly simple.

When you get to the spot where you want a cocoon, stop (with more experience, you will be able to just slow down) and while maintaining a hold with your front hand so the twist doesn't travel down into the fiber supply, draft backward with your back hand **(STEP 1)**. Then, pinch after this predrafted section with your front hand pinkie finger **(STEP 2)** so you can predraft a second pull **(STEP 3)**. You should now have several inches of predrafted fiber containing no twist. Now test it by spinning past the predrafted fiber **(STEP 4)**. Is it thinner than the section of yarn before and after it? If it isn't, try again. These several inches need to be thinner than the yarn surrounding them, or when you put in a cocoon, it won't stay like it should.

Spin thinner under cocoons.

*Twist accumulates in the thin spots,
holding the cocoon in place.*

Building the cocoon Once you have the predrafting sorted out and you are sure it is really thinner than the surrounding singles, you are ready to build the cocoon. Predraft twice, then move a bit into the predrafted section and let twist accumulate. This is to make sure that you're well within the thin section when you start your cocoon. It is very important that the top and bottom of the cocoon be anchored in the thin section of the singles. Gently slide the index finger of your front/drafting hand up through the predrafted fibers, splitting them into two delicate halves **(STEP 5)**. Now take the cocoon fiber you've set aside and insert the tip of one end into the split you've made, creating a tiny fiber sandwich **(STEP 6)**. That is the top anchor and, as long as it accumulates twist, it is solid.

Let the twist travel through the anchor all the way to your front/drafting pinkie, which should be lightly pinching the end of the predrafted section against your hand to keep the twist from getting into the fiber supply. You will build the cocoon between the top anchor—where you inserted the tip of the cocoon fiber—and your pinkie, making sure the twist doesn't go farther.

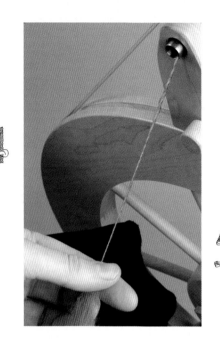

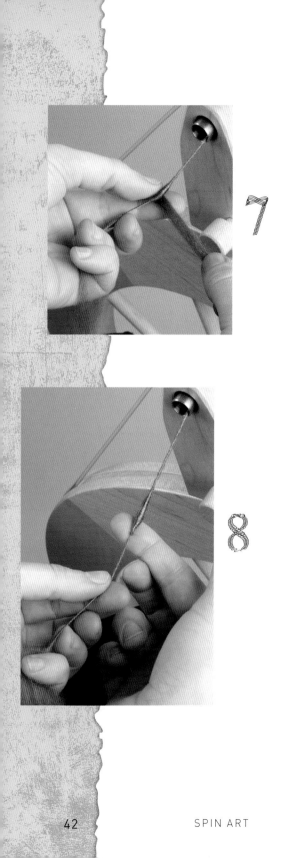

If you have stopped treadling, start again slowly. Twist will be entering the predrafted fibers. Now you're going to build the bulk of the cocoon by corespinning. Hold the cocoon fiber out to the side at a 90-degree angle and corespin onto the singles in your front hand. It helps to use the thumb and index finger of your front hand to turn the cocoon as you build it so that you wrap the cocoon's fibers around each other tightly, like wrapping a bandage around a limb **(STEP 7)**. To form a cocoon shape, build more fiber up in the middle and taper down to the end. When you are ready to finalize the cocoon, twist the cocoon fiber like you are turning a lock in a key so you've got a smaller point where it spins on. If you are using a protein fiber (such as wool), the bottom anchor of the cocoon is easy because the fiber wants to stick to itself. Since all it takes to make that happen is the accumulation of some twist, just spin the tip of the cocoon fiber right onto the tip of the cocoon and you are done **(STEP 8)**. If you're using a cellulose fiber or some other slick material that lacks scales to make it stick, break off your fiber supply and do a worsted join just barely over the tip of the cocoon. Make sure to then draft together the fiber supply and the singles that is sticking out a bit from the end of the cocoon **(STEP 9)**.

Chances are, when you are learning (and even sometimes when you're not) you will overspin the singles yarn while you build the cocoon. To correct this, just draft out some of your singles fiber without treadling and let the twist redistribute. Most of the time this will take care of overspinning, even if you have to get up and walk across the room to get the yarn long enough to eat up all that extra twist.

tailspinning

If you're aiming to whip up a wild yarn with lavish texture, or if you have a pile of locks you don't know what to do with, tailspinning is an excellent and daring approach. Though it still falls under the heading of corespinning, this technique is so named because of the materials used and the appearance of the resulting yarn—highly textured with tips of locks hanging loose.

TIPS FOR TECHNIQUE: introduce twist into commercially spun yarn for better balance (see page 16); basic corespinning (see page 34).

fiber

Core Tailspinning, like the other forms of corespinning, employs a core, and all guidelines regarding the core for corespinning hold true for tailspinning as well. It will serve the yarn well, especially if you do not want it terribly overspun, to read "Introduce twist into commercially spun yarn for better balance" in the Tips section (page 16).

Locks This technique only works if you use intact or partially intact locks. Combed or carded locks can be corespun and do make lovely yarns, but they won't work for tailspinning. Fibers such as young mohair, Bluefaced Leicester, and suri alpaca will give you a soft but defined tailspun yarn and can be spun from a mass of fiber without the locks being separated. Dig into your stash or seek out some silky washed locks and get ready for a yarn that looks more like the sheep it came from than any you've spun before.

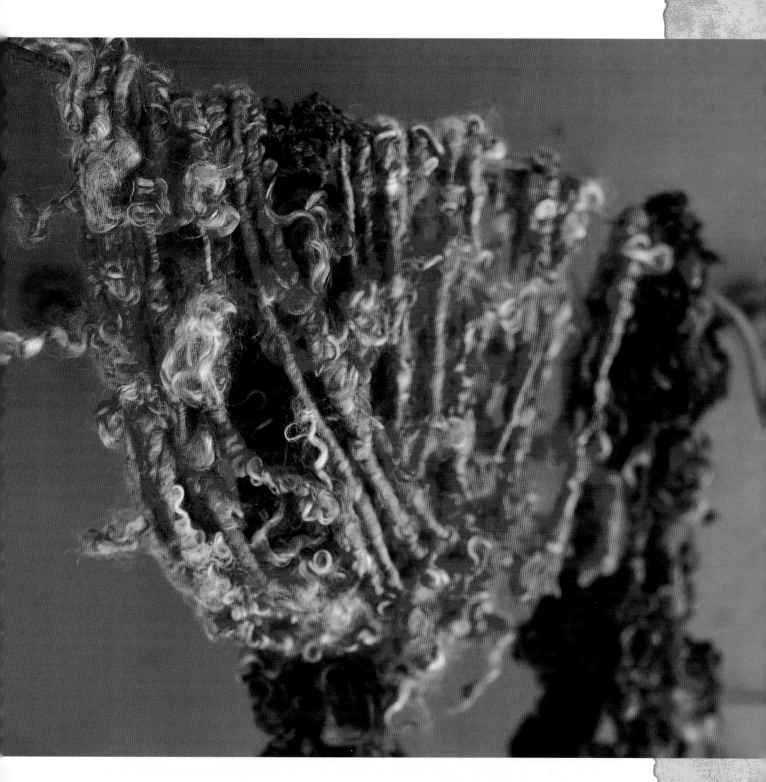

wheel setup

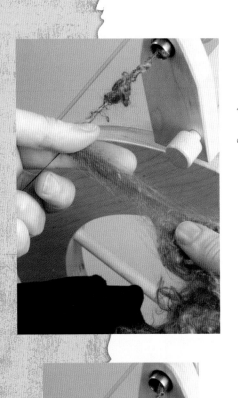

Because the fiber stays in the form of locks, this yarn is inevitably bulky and does not need much twist. Set up your wheel to go as slow as it can (pick your biggest pulley), with a considerable amount of tension but not so much that it is ripping the yarn out of your hands. Place the core at your feet on the same side as your drafting/front hand and get ready to spin in whatever direction you choose.

The sample yarn is kid mohair locks on a 2-ply wool core with S-twist added before the yarn is tailspun in the Z direction.

spinning

Hold a mass of soft, silky, teased locks in your fiber-supply/back hand and reach in with your drafting/front hand and start corespinning **(STEP 1)**. So far, this is just basic corespinning; the difference lies in the fiber and in the next step—extracting the tips. This happens in two ways and at two different times. The first way is while a lock is in the process of being corespun. If you see the tip once you have attached the lock, grab it and pull it free from the core, out of the spin so it hangs loose. The second way catches the locks that you miss the first time: as soon as you corespin a bit of the fiber on the core, check to see whether you can spot any locks. You have to do this before you add too much twist because they are harder to pull out if they're bundled down, and you also must do this before you add more fiber, which has the potential to cover up the tips already on your core. When you see one (or as often as you like), grab the intact tip and carefully pull it away from the core, letting it hang loose **(STEP 2)**. These silky locks may not have the length and drama of their longer, coarser brothers, but they are soft, textured, and easier to work up.

The slowness of the technique and the bulkiness of the finished product give you plenty of opportunity to appreciate the natural beauty of the fiber, something we love so much preserved in a unique handspun yarn.

extreme tailspinning

If you love long wools, this is the technique for you. Using locks that hang lustrously in 6-inch, 8-inch, or even 12-inch spirals, this is tailspinning taken to the extreme. Also, if you have one, this might be the time to break out your bulky flyer or bigger orifice.

TIPS FOR TECHNIQUE: introduce twist into commercially spun yarn for better balance (see page 16); basic corespinning (see page 34).

fiber

Core Extreme tailspinning, like the other forms of corespinning, employs a core, and all guidelines regarding the core for corespinning hold true for this technique as well.

Locks Cotswold, Teeswater, Lincoln, Wensleydale—any of the long, luster wools will work for this technique. Intact locks have two ends: the butt end (which was attached to the sheep) and the tip (which should taper to a point for the longwool breeds). Spin this yarn true to the locks' original arrangement on the sheep, with the butt ends attached to the core and the tips floating free. Separate the locks from each other, making sure the butt end is opened up a bit by teasing it out with your fingers, a hand picker, or dog brush. Lay them out with the tips facing one direction so that it is easy

to grab one after another (STEP 1). This takes a bit of time, but you will appreciate not having to stop spinning every few minutes to do it as you go.

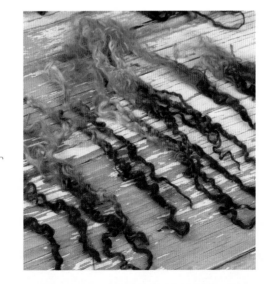

1

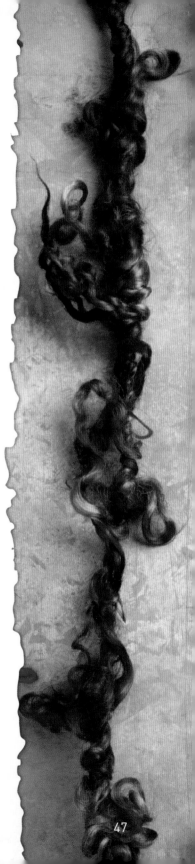

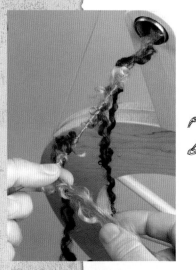

wheel setup

Even more so than basic tailspinning, this yarn is a bulky one and does not need much twist. If you have a bulky or plying head for your wheel, this is the time to use it. Set up your wheel to go as slowly as it can (pick your biggest pulley), with as much tension as possible while still giving you control. Place the core at your feet on the same side as your drafting/front hand, and get ready to spin in whatever direction you choose.

The sample yarn is Teeswater locks on a 2-ply wool core with S-twist added before the yarn is tailspun in the Z direction.

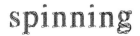

spinning

Grab a lock with your back hand and corespin the butt end onto the core **(STEP 2)**. Attach the lock for at least 1 inch and as much as several inches, depending on the length of the yarn and the shape of the lock, and stop when it is well attached and about ½ inch before you like the look of the remaining lock that is hanging loose. Now, without releasing your drafting hand's hold on the lock's core, grab another lock with your back/fiber-supply hand and corespin its butt end together with the already attached lock for about ½ inch. Attach it above the tip of the lock hanging loose **(STEP 3)**. Now cross the lock you're currently spinning over the previous lock spun, which should be arranged farther up the core, farther from your body, so that the new lock is now closer to your body **(STEP 4)**. Continue to spin the second lock until you like the look of it, then pick up a third lock and spin it the same way. It is slow going, but you will see a wild, textured, tailspun yarn start to fill your bobbin.

bumps

We spinners spend lots of time treadling toward perfection. Early on, we experience bumpy, uneven yarn and spend a great deal of time trying to rectify it. Brace yourself—these bumps are different. These are bumps you want.

In this chapter, you'll learn to spin two different bumpy singles yarns: thick-and-thin and beehives. Thick-and-thin is quite basic, but can also be one of the hardest techniques to grasp, particularly for experienced spinners. Beehives are a type of coil. They are fairly involved and will keep your fingers both busy and tired, but when you are done, your eyes will be wide and your mouth agape.

Both bumpy yarns rely on short- to medium-staple fibers and a short forward or short backward draw. While both yarns adhere to the rules of fiber and spinning, each has hand mechanics that fall outside defined spinning categories and pave a bumpy road all their own.

techniques in this chapter | thick-and-thin • beehives

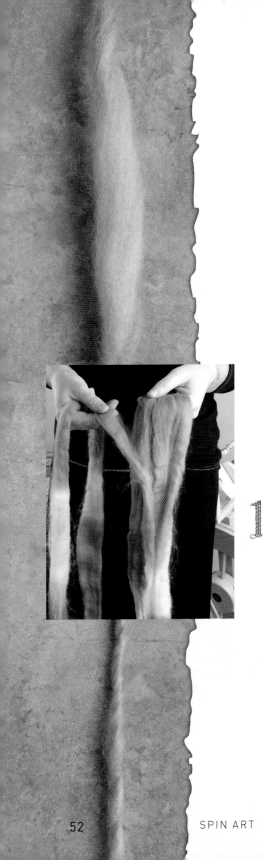

thick-and-thin

I know what you're thinking: Thick-and-thin, that's what I spun as a beginner—let's get to the hard stuff! To that I reply, This *is* the hard stuff! A good thick-and-thin yarn can be deceptively difficult, and it seems that the better spinner you are, the harder it is to master. After spinning bobbin after bobbin in the pursuit of thin, even yarn, it feels a bit sacrilegious to intentionally spin an uneven yarn. You can do it, though, and do it in a way that is far beyond the thick-and-thin you spun when you first put foot to treadle. This durable thick-and-thin singles yarn is going to have style and intent, and though as a singles yarn it can't really be balanced, it will hang in a more balanced-looking way than any singles yarn you have ever seen.

fiber

Start with a combed top of short or medium staple—something like Merino or Targhee wool. (Short cellulose fibers work well, too, but save those until you've got the hang of it.) The thick sections should be rather short, and long fibers make that difficult. For the thick sections to have integrity, they must be just a tad shorter than the staple length of the fiber. Long staple lengths tend to diminish the drama of the thick-and-thin effect, and make it unwieldy to spin. I like to use variegated or painted top, but whatever you choose, make sure it is nice and fluffy, not at all felted or matted. Separate the fiber into strips about the width of your thumb **(STEP 1)**, but don't predraft or attenuate the fibers; they need to stay aligned so you get consistent thickness and shape. These thumb-width strips are about twice as thick as the thick sections in your yarn are going to be. Keep this in mind for future adjustments.

wheel setup

While it is possible to execute this technique as rapidly as your wheel will allow, I recommend going slowly your first time. Set the tension for a light to medium uptake to give twist time to enter the thin-and-thick sections before it is pulled in. If you notice, however, that the thin sections kink up before they disappear into the orifice, increase the tension a wee bit. If you are using a bobbin-led wheel, try taking your brake band all the way off for this yarn or lacing it between the hooks. This yarn can be spun in either direction.

The sample yarn is spun in the Z direction from Merino combed top.

spinning

Attach and spin a few yards evenly. This thick-and-thin uses a modified inchworm, a short backward draft, and a nifty wrist twist. When you're ready to spin a thick section, gently pinch the whole width of the strip of fiber with the outside flat of your thumb on your front/drafting hand **(STEP 2)**. Now rotate that hand as if you are turning a key in a lock **(STEP 3)**. What your wrist twist just pulled forward is the whole thick section. Where it thins out will be the start of the thin section. Glide your drafting hand gently over the thick section **(STEP 4)**, being careful not to take any of the fibers with you, and pinch right before it gets thin again **(STEP 5)**. Continue and spin a length of thin by drawing your fiber-supply hand in a short backward draw while your front hand controls the twist **(STEP 6)**. Pinch down with your thumb again, twist your wrist, and pull the fiber back to create another thick section.

With a short fiber, these thick sections do not need much twist to stay together. If you use the above method, the thick sections will be just a bit shorter than the staple length. This allows the ends of most of the fibers to be trapped in the high-twist thin sections at either end and keeps the thick sections from drifting apart, despite having very little twist. If the thick sections are longer than the staple length, there is nothing to keep them from drifting apart since no end fibers are trapped in high twist sections. So keep the thick sections shorter than the staple length and be aware that there should be a notable difference between the thick-and-thin sections. These factors are key to ensuring the sturdiness of your thick-and-thin yarn.

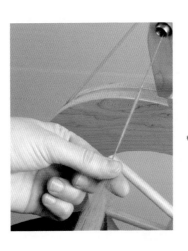

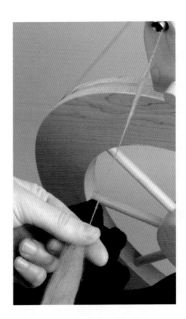

This yarn is more likely to pill than some others because of its dearth of twist, but its uniqueness and softness make up for this. But don't think it is delicate just because it's not super hard wearing. Give it a tug. If you have spun the thick portions the right length, it will stay together handsomely, giving you a soft, squishy thick-and-thin yarn with a good amount of integrity. After you wind it off and tie it, hang it in a loop, and you will be amazed: because of its thick untwisted sections, this yarn almost breaks the rule that a singles yarn can't be truly balanced.

How staple length stabilizes thick-and-thin.

If staple length is shorter than thick sections, fibers can easily drift or be pulled apart.

Thick sections should be shorter than staple length so fiber ends get locked in place.

a word about the wrist twist

My own failed attempts to teach spinners to spin thick-and-thin led me to pick apart my own technique, and I discovered that I unconsciously do this little thing with my wrist. As soon as I started teaching the wrist twist, thick-and-thin seemed to come much more easily to even the most even of spinners. It seems like a small thing, but it really is the key. Pinching the whole strip and then rotating your wrist forces you to draft all of the fibers at once, ensuring that the thick sections are uniform and as thick as can be. This keeps your hands and their movement-memory from minimizing the thickness, giving this control instead to the wrist twist. Hands that are used to drafting and spinning evenly get a consistent reminder that they are doing something different.

beehives

Since the first coil was spun and subsequently written about,[1] coiling has been a plying technique. It has evolved, gotten more elaborate and sophisticated, but has remained something to be accomplished in the plying stage of yarn making.

At some point, I was issued a personal challenge by one of my workshop students to "spin a stable coil in a singles yarn," and the coil evolved yet again. After months of experimentation, a fat, happy coil burst mysteriously forth from a singles yarn. The beehive was born.

Many textured yarn techniques can be sped up to normal or near-normal speed once they are mastered. This is not one of them. Beehives take plenty of time, finger adeptness, and patience to learn, and even when you've gotten good at them, they will still be slow going. But I think you will find that it is worth it.

TIPS FOR TECHNIQUE: cocoons (see page 39); basic corespinning (see page 34).

fiber

For both the base singles, any fiber and fiber preparation will work. For the beehive fiber, short- or medium-staple fiber will give you the best results. In the learning stages, I recommend wool: it just makes things easier because of its natural grabbiness. Once you've got an understanding of the mechanics of this technique, try different materials for both components. Cotton makes especially fantastic beehives.

It will save a smidge of time if you prepare the beehive fiber by making several mustache-like bundles. Also, take a moment to neaten up these fibers by rolling them in your hands or on your leg. You will not be drafting them, and the more the fibers remain together, the easier the spinning process will be **(STEP 1)**.

---

[1] Diane Varney (*Spinning Designer Yarns*, Interweave, 1976), then Lexi Boeger (*Handspun Revolution*, 2005), and then Symeon North (*Get Spun*, Interweave, 2010).

wheel setup

This yarn does not need much twist, but beehive construction is hindered by strong uptake, so it's necessary to choose a bigger pulley than you would use for the singles and to slow your treadling a bit. Uptake should be set slightly lower than medium so that while your hands are building the beehives, you don't have to also keep the yarn from disappearing into the orifice. This yarn can be spun in either direction.

The sample yarn is spun in the Z direction out of Bluefaced Leicester. The beehives are Merino and silk.

spinning

Start by spinning a singles, remembering that, since it is going to remain a singles, it will not require as much twist as it would if you were going to ply.

Predrafting under the beehive As with cocoons, the beehive's structure lies in basic spinning mechanics. So it requires that we predraft a section of the singles over which the beehive will be spun. For a more detailed explanation of why this is important, how it works, and exactly how to predraft under the beehive, please go back and read "Predrafting Under the Cocoon" on page 40. When you are comfortable with this preliminary predrafting, go ahead and create several inches of predrafted fiber that contains no twist.

Building the beehive With the predrafted section in your hands, slide your front/drafting hand in until you are well within the thin section. When you start a beehive, it is really important that the top and bottom of the beehive be anchored in the thin section of the singles. With the index finger of your front hand, slide it gently up through the predrafted fibers, splitting them into two delicate halves (STEP 2). Now, insert the tip of one end of the beehive fiber into the split you have made, creating a tiny fiber sandwich (STEP 3). That is the top anchor, and as long as it accumulates twist, it is solid. Let go of the fiber supply with your back/fiber-supply hand. Remember: you're still refraining from treadling. With the hand that just let go of the fiber supply, grab the other end of the beehive fiber and start to twirl it (STEP 4) in the same direction that you are spinning your singles (this will be the same direction the wheel is spinning). Imagine twirling a tendril of your hair around a finger; it's the same action. Now, slowly begin to treadle, and while holding the twisted beehive fiber out at a 70- to 90-degree angle (as if you were corespinning), let a bit of it wind on and around the singles that is now accumulating twist (STEP 5). Once the twist you put into the beehive fiber is gone, stop treadling and twirl it again. Treadle and wind it on, continuing this process until all but the tippiest tip of beehive fiber is not wound onto the singles yarn (STEP 6). The bigger and longer your beehive fiber, the more times you will have to stop, twirl, start, wind on. While holding your singles yarn with your front/drafting hand, push the beehive fiber you've just wrapped around the singles yarn gently toward the orifice so that it squishes into a beehive shape (STEP 7).

You have anchored the top and created a beehive. All that is left is to anchor the bottom of the beehive so all your hard work does not fall out. As long as you have some thin singles yarn left, it's easy. Break the singles fiber off close to the end of the beehive (STEP 8), slightly untwist the end of the singles, and reattach the fiber by just letting a few of the fibers catch, at about a 45-degree angle, over the end of the beehive, creating a worsted join (STEP 9). Be sure to then draft the end of the singles fiber together with the fiber supply so that it creates a stable join.

Even with the wheel set up on a slightly slower pulley than would typically be required for the singles, it is likely that you have overspun the yarn around the beehive. To correct this, draft out some of the singles fiber without treadling and let the twist redistribute (STEP 10).

I'd end with a quippy *That's it!* but I realize that this technique is slow, fiddly, and features a lot of stopping and starting. Keep at it: once you have it down, your beehives will mystify your fellow spinners.

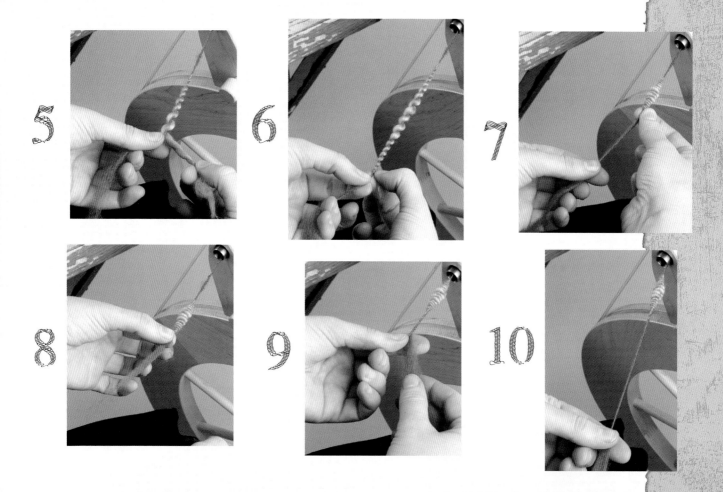

foreign objects

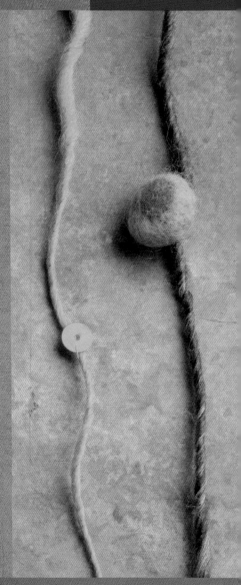

When people think of "art yarn," they envision yarn with stuff in it. Hopefully, you're beginning to see that textured yarn is much more than that, but it is also true that "yarn with stuff in it" falls squarely within the realm of textured yarn. Foreign objects can be as simple as tiny seed beads, as dramatic as handfelted baubles, or as extreme as baby-doll heads. Whether they fall into the beautiful or shocking category for you, foreign objects can be great fun to spin.

Both the techniques here give you a full range of creativity by working with absolutely any fiber and any fiber preparation. They also lend themselves to different drafting styles. Short forward or backward draw may facilitate learning the techniques, but don't stop there. Integrating foreign objects can be paired with long draw and corespinning. Also, yarns from both techniques can easily be turned into plied yarns.

This chapter covers two ways to put foreign objects in yarn: stringing and integrating. It also discusses the benefits and limitations of both methods. So take a few deep breaths and leave your reservations behind. You are about to put some stuff in yarn.

techniques in this chapter | stringing • integrating

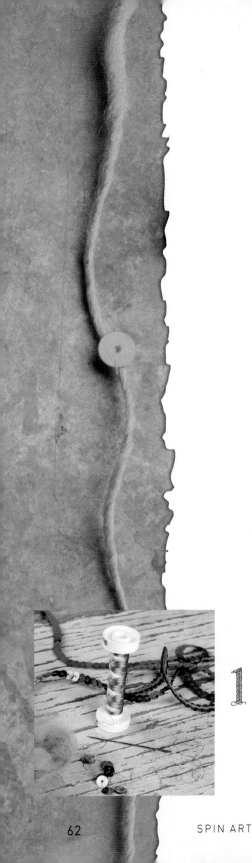

stringing

The proper method for incorporating foreign objects is dictated by the object itself. This method is perfect for adding subtle objects such as small beads, sequins, and other small, light objects. But it is not a very effective way to insert large or heavy objects, since such objects tend to cause conditions I call "bead hammock" or "open triangles." Stringing is a very simple technique for incorporating foreign objects, and if you have mastered the racing stripe, it will be a breeze.

Stringing conditions to avoid.

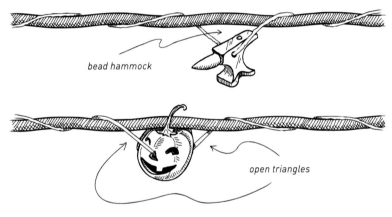

bead hammock

open triangles

TIPS FOR TECHNIQUE: racing stripe (see page 22).

fiber

The base of this yarn is a singles, and any fiber and fiber prep will work. The racing stripe can be commercially spun or handspun, but make sure that it is both thin enough to string your foreign objects of choice and strong enough to take the weight of the objects you are including.

Once you have chosen and gathered the base fiber, racing stripe, and foreign objects, use a needle to string enough foreign objects for the entire bobbin of yarn onto the racing stripe **(STEP 1)**.

Arrange your loaded racing stripe strand at your feet on your front/drafting hand side.

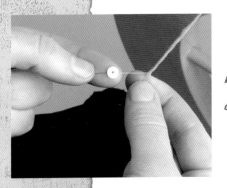

wheel setup

This technique does not dictate the setup of your wheel, so set up for the singles you will be spinning. You can spin in either direction, but if you have spun your own racing stripe, spin in the direction opposite to the stripe.

The sample yarn is a singles of Polwarth combed top spun Z, with a silk thread strung with 100 single sequins.

spinning

For this technique, you will spin a racing stripe—a singles that is spun using a short backward (or forward) draw while wrapping it with a prespun yarn. The difference here is that a collection of foreign objects is suspended between your bobbin/cone of racing stripe on the floor and your front/drafting hand.

Join the fiber to the leader and begin spinning a racing stripe. When you are ready to insert a foreign object, reach down and grab one with your front/drafting hand (STEP 2). Bring it up to the drafting triangle and spin past it (STEP 3). Continue until you have filled the bobbin or run with fiber, racing stripe, or foreign objects. If the objects you are spinning in are small and light enough, you shouldn't need to anchor them. If they are big and heavy, you should incorporate them more securely with the integrating technique (see page 65). There you have it: you've officially spun stuff into your handspun.

variation: strung and plied

If you'd prefer a plied yarn to a singles yarn with a racing stripe, it is just as easy. Simply string your foreign objects onto a commercial or handspun singles, then ply it with another singles as you would a traditional 2-ply. Whenever you want to include a foreign object, grab one, bring it up, and ply right past it. Again, if the objects you're using are not too big or heavy, they will stay where you put them.

integrating

Hands down, this is my favorite way to securely and permanently integrate foreign objects into a yarn. It is easy, flawless (there's no bead hammock or open triangle), versatile, allows you to spin in any manner you want (front draft, back draft, corespinning), and when you are done, you can even ply it if you are so inclined. Sadly, it doesn't work for all types of foreign objects; but when it does work, it puts in overtime.

fiber

Foreign objects that can be integrated include anything that has a hole (beads, buttons) and anything than can be made to have a hole (handfelted baubles, silk cocoons).

Any fiber and preparation will work beautifully. You will also need long, thin strips of fiber that matches your main fiber and a sharp large-eyed needle. Using the needle, thread the foreign objects onto the strips of fiber **(STEP 1)**. Once you have several strung on a strip, carefully and evenly distribute the objects, leaving about 2 inches between each. Now, gently separate each foreign object so that each one has about 1 inch of fiber coming out of each side **(STEP 2)**.

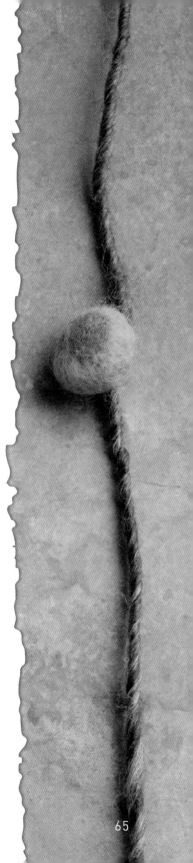

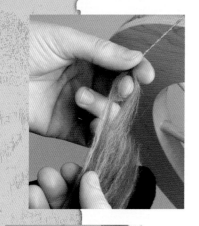

wheel setup

Set up your wheel for the singles you will be spinning. Keep in mind that thin yarns should be paired with lighter foreign objects so the yarn doesn't drag under its weight. Thicker yarns can handle heavier objects. This singles can be spun in either direction.

The sample yarn is spun Z out of Merino and rose combed top, with needlefelted wool beads that were run through the washing machine.

spinning

Start spinning the singles in whatever drafting style you choose. When you are ready for a foreign object, use the index finger on your front/drafting hand to poke gently upward and split the fiber in the drafting triangle into two halves **(STEP 3)**. Now, grab one of the fiber-strung foreign objects, insert the fiber's tip into the split **(STEP 4)**, and draft it with the fiber supply. This is very important: if you do not draft the two sets of fiber together, the foreign object won't be integrated into the yarn, and it won't be as stable and secure. So, draft the fibers together until you reach the foreign object, then spin right past it **(STEP 5)**, still drafting the fibers together. Now the foreign object is a part of the yarn.

off-center threading

If you are poking holes into foreign objects yourself, do not go through the center. Thread them as close to the edge as possible while still making them secure. You use this off-center threading so, when the yarn is worked into fabric, there's no bump on the back side where half your bauble resides and, instead, the back is flat and most of your bauble is on the front of your fabric (see step 1 photo, page 65).

part two

PLIED TECHNIQUES

bumps

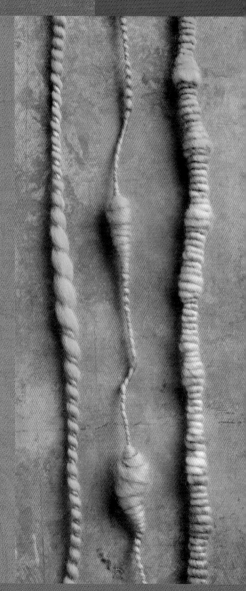

Bumps, bumps, bumps. You tried them out in the singles section of the book, and now you're moving up. These bumps are made during the plying process and are a textured yarn spinner's bread and butter. Some of the most popular and mysterious of all textured spinning techniques are plied bumps. They will challenge your hands, bring a smile to your face, and confound your spinning friends.

All but one of the techniques—coils, allow for any fiber and any fiber preparation; but all employ uneven tensioning during plying. In fact, that's the secret to bumps: holding one ply straight out from the orifice while the other ply careens way out to the side at something akin to a 90-degree angle. You will learn each technique's sequence of events and particular anchoring needs. And you will learn which plied bump techniques can be balanced (all but one) and how to reach that perfect state.

This chapter delves into five different plied techniques, each featuring a different kind of bump. The first, and easiest, is the spiral ply. Don't let that fool you, though: it gets tougher from there. Also included is an age-old favorite, the stack, and something new and fun, the stack trap. Finally, you will see two coiling techniques that will stretch your fingers and skills, leaving you with a sense of accomplishment and delight.

techniques in this chapter | spiral plying • stacks • stack traps • supercoils • coils

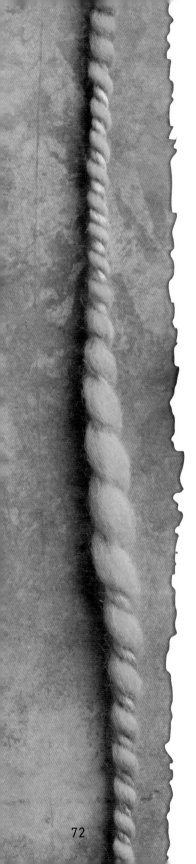

spiral plying

This simple technique can make a standout yarn and get you ready for more complicated plying. Spiral plying is about as easy as textured yarn gets, but is fundamental for many techniques. It is essentially uneven plying, but there are several elements you can vary to spice it up: the fiber content of both plies, the angle at which you hold both plies, and the thickness and evenness of the plies. So, while it may seem almost too easy to tackle, take a few skeins and try your hand at it. You will likely end up with finer hand control and some gorgeous yarns.

TIPS FOR TECHNIQUE: introduce twist into commercially spun yarn for better balance (see page 16).

singles

You will need two singles yarns for spiral plying: one thick or thick-and-thin, and the other thinner and even. Any fiber and fiber preparation will work for both plies. The thinner, even singles yarn can be commercially spun, but if you go that route, please read "Introduce twist into commercially spun yarn for better balance" in the Tips section. The handspun singles yarn should have enough twist to get a nice ply in the opposite direction. The handspun singles yarn that will be spiraling around the other should have roughly 10 percent more yardage.

Place the singles yarn you want to spiral at your feet on your back/fiber-supply hand side and the thin, even singles on the other side.

wheel setup

Nothing in this technique should slow you down, so set up your wheel as if you were going to evenly ply the thicker of your two singles yarns. Spin in the opposite direction of your singles.

The sample yarn uses a solid combed Merino top spun a bit thick-and-thin and variegated Merino and silk combed top spun thin. Both singles yarns are spun Z, and spiral plied S.

plying

Attach both singles yarns to your leader, holding the thin singles yarn in one hand and the thicker singles yarn in your other hand. Hold the thinner yarn, with tension, straight out from the orifice and the thicker yarn, with less tension, to the side at somewhere between a 45- and 90-degree angle (STEP 1). Start treadling and ply the two singles together by letting the thicker singles wrap around the thinner one (STEP 2). That's all there is to it. Make sure you put in enough ply twist to balance the yarn and give you the look you want. To further expand this yarn's possibilities, experiment with the angle at which you hold the wrapping yarn and at which the yarn wraps around the other.

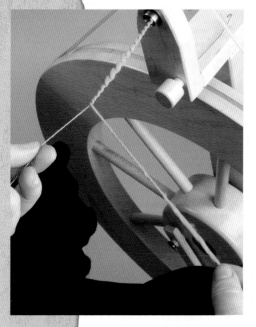

1

2

stacks

This technique has been around a long time but continues to delight spinners and knitters alike. It is an easy, fun way to add isolated spots of texture in otherwise traditional yarns. I often call stacks "poor man's coils," because they are much easier to execute than coils but can look strikingly similar. These knots or stacks made during the plying process can be small and subdued or big and dramatic and the same color as your yarn or a different color—it's up to you.

singles

You will need two singles for this yarn of any fiber, preparation, and weight; but it will work out best if neither is drastically uneven. If you want your stacks to stand out in a different color or fiber (like the sample yarn), when you're spinning your singles, break off your main fiber, spin 2- to 4-inch sections of your contrasting fiber, then go back to your main fiber. Do this as often as you want stacks to appear.

Both singles should have enough single twist to get a nice ply in the opposite direction.

Place one singles yarn on each side of you, at your feet. If you are using bobbins of handspun but don't have two lazy kates, putting a ball in a bowl works well.

wheel setup

Set up your wheel for plying the two singles. When you come to a place where you want a stack, you'll need to slow down your treadling. But overall you should be able to spin at a pace suitable to plying the singles you spun. Spin in the opposite direction of your singles.

The sample yarn is two Merino and silk singles spun Z and plied S. Both are gray and handspun, but one is spun with 3-inch sections of pink silk. Those pink sections are then plied into stacks.

plying

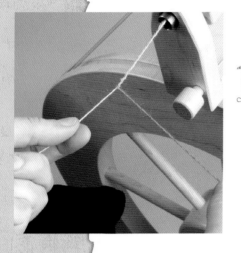

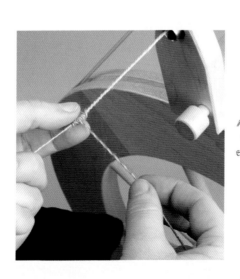

Join the two singles yarns to the leader and start plying (traditional or spiral will work). When you are ready to build a stack, slow your treadling down a bit, pull the singles yarn you want the stack to be built from out to the side at a 70- to 90-degree angle (STEP 1). Slide your other hand up to where the plies meet—the plying triangle (STEP 2). Wind the singles yarn pulled out to the side back up on the yarn you just plied, using your other hand to help it wrap tightly, like wrapping a bandage on an arm (STEP 3). Build up and down over the same space to build the stack. Be sure to wrap it up and down. Don't jump from the top to the bottom because it is more likely to come undone. When you get to the bottom of the stack and you are happy with its shape and tightness, switch tension by bringing the singles yarn you made the stack out of back to center. Pull the other singles yarn out to the other side, letting it wind on once or twice (STEP 4) to anchor it. In building the stack, it is likely you have overplied the yarn, so go ahead and ply the next few inches without treadling to redistribute the twist. Now, continue your regular plying until you want another stack.

You have abundant choices for spinning stacks: they can be long or short, thick in the middle and tapered on the ends, messy or neat, the same color as the yarn or a contrasting color. Experiment until you achieve the effect you want.

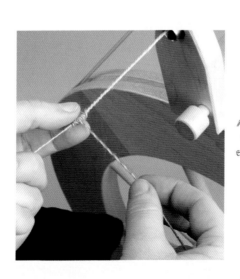

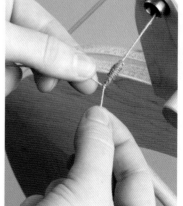

stack traps

With the addition of just a few bits of contrasting fiber, you can turn a regular stack into a fabulous and effective stack trap. A stack trap is a stack that traps something (fiber, most likely) beneath it. While the technique is similar to that for regular stacks, the final look of the yarn is quite different.

TIPS FOR TECHNIQUE: stacks (see page 75).

singles

You'll need two singles yarns for this yarn of any fiber, preparation, and weight; but it will work out best if neither is drastically uneven You will also need some contrasting fiber to trap: cotton and short-staple wools work great for this.

Both singles should have enough single twist to get a nice ply in the opposite direction.

Place one singles yarn on each side of you, at your feet.

wheel setup

Set up your wheel for plying your two singles. Spin in the opposite direction of your singles.

The sample yarn is Merino and silk with bits of cotton trapped under the stacks.

plying

Join the yarns to the leader and ply evenly until you want to add a stack trap, then arrange your singles so that one is held with tension, straight out from the orifice, and the other is off to the side at a 70- to 90-degree angle. Place the contrasting bundle of fiber on the tensioned singles yarn as if it is a part of it (STEP 1). Now, build the stack over the top of both the contrasting fiber and the yarn (STEP 2). Be sure to go over the edges of the fiber bundle for stability and neatness. That's it. If you can master stacks, you can use them to trap foreign objects.

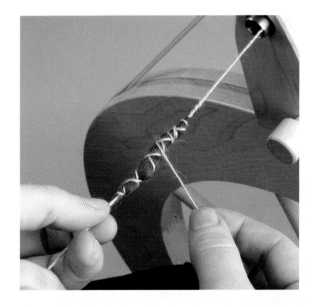

supercoils

The supercoil is a spectacular technique that yields yarn full of texture and whimsy. I consistently find that spinners are amazed at how complex it looks, but how easily it is accomplished. As impressive looking and easy as it is, the trade-off is that it is hard to balance and does not have great drape or hand. Its drawbacks become benefits, however, since the lack of drape and hand work together with the thick texture to prevent the lack of balance from biasing when knit. So go ahead and give these coils a try. You'll think they are super. Plus, they get you ready for more difficult coils to come.

TIPS FOR TECHNIQUE: spiral plying (see page 72); introduce twist into commercially spun yarn for better balance (see page 16).

singles

While any fiber and prep will work for these singles, multicolored fibers especially come alive, as do multifiber carded batts. You need two bobbins of singles. The one that will be coiled should not be too thin, should have a plenty of yardage, and should have lots of single twist in it. Since the length of the finished supercoils is actually the multiplied thickness of the singles, the thicker the singles yarn is, the more yardage of supercoils you will get: and the more twist in your singles, the closer your supercoils will be to balanced.

Yarn spinner Sarah Anderson created a technique where you load your core singles onto a suspended spindle to allow the twist to dissipate as you coil. This makes the supercoil yarn much easier to balance. If you love supercoiled yarns, do look it up!

How supercoils stack up.

thinner single

*more wraps required
to go a given length*

thicker single

*fewer wraps required
to go a given length*

The other singles yarn will not be seen at all and, in fact, will act more like a core. Feel free to use any strong fiber for it. You can use commercially spun laceweight but be sure to introduce opposite twist into it to help with balance (see Tips section). You can also use a barely spun singles yarn, spun in the opposite direction of your coiling singles yarn. When you ply, you'll be adding more twist to the core while taking twist out of the coiling singles yarn.

Place the coiling singles at your feet so that you can hold it in your back/fiber-supply hand and the core on the other side so that you can hold it with your front/drafting hand.

wheel setup

The mechanics of creating super-coils—taking lots of yards of a singles yarn and squishing them together into a few coiled yards—can create a very overspun yarn. If you have 200 yards of twist and you squish it into 75 yards, that's 125 yards of extra twist. To counteract this, set your wheel on its slowest pulley, with a strong uptake. Ply in the opposite direction of the coiling singles yarn.

The sample yarn is Z-spun from Optim Merino combed top for the coiling yarn and a lightly S-spun silk and Merino singles as the core. The yarn is plied in the S direction.

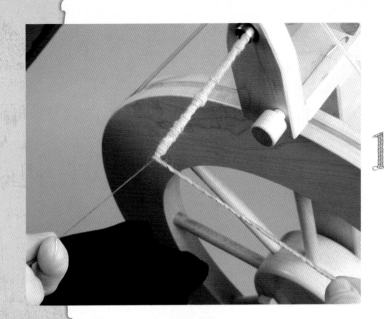

plying

Join the yarns to the leader and ply evenly for a few inches. Now, with your back/fiber-supply hand, pull the coiling singles out to the side at a 70- to 90-degree angle. The core should remain straight out from the orifice, held in your front/drafting hand. Slow your treadling and let the coiling singles wrap around the core as if you are spiral plying **(STEP 1)**. Each time your spiral plying covers the core up to where your hand is holding the core, use the hand holding the coiling singles yarn to gently push the spirals up until they touch and completely cover the core **(STEP 2)**. There's a sweet spot here: you should push up until it just covers the core. Don't be tempted to push up as far as you can because you will make the yarn harder and less balanced. Do, however, push the coiling singles yarn up enough that it is not sliding around. Once you have pushed it up, slide your front/drafting hand a bit down the core **(STEP 3)** and start spiral plying again, then push it up. Continue in this manner until you have used up the coiling singles yarn. Don't be surprised if you triple the thickness and lose about 60 percent of the yardage in this technique. But the 40 percent you do keep will be 100 percent awesome.

coils

The coil is a definite crowd-pleaser and a pleasure to spin, and if spun correctly with attention to technique, a joy to work. You're about to spin a coil that is soft, balanced, and thanks to two easy-ish anchors, does not move around.

TIPS FOR TECHNIQUE: thick-and-thin (see page 52); spiral plying (see page 72); introduce twist into commercially spun yarn for better balance (see page 16).

singles

Like all the techniques in this section, much of what makes a coil a coil is in the plying. However, if we neglect proper preparation of the base singles, the coils won't have the stability and durability that a usable yarn requires. So, before you try this technique, head back to the thick-and-thin chapter and master it. But when you generate a thick-and-thin singles for making coils, overspin it. You won't see much more twist accumulate in the thick sections, but you'll notice that if you release the tension a bit, the thin sections will start to kink. Don't worry: that's what you want for this technique. A coil will introduce extra twist in the plying direction, plus

the singles must have enough single twist to reconcile the fact that we'll be squishing all that extra twist into a shorter length of yarn. The more twist you can put in the original singles, the better: try for a yarn with a twist angle of 12 to 17 degrees in the thick sections and 40 to 45 degrees in the thin section. Also, keep in mind that the coils are going to be about the thickness of the thick sections, but they will be firmer, so if the fit is tight for the thick sections through the orifice, it will be even tighter for the coils. Adjust accordingly by stripping your fiber out a bit thinner when you make the thick-and-thin yarn.

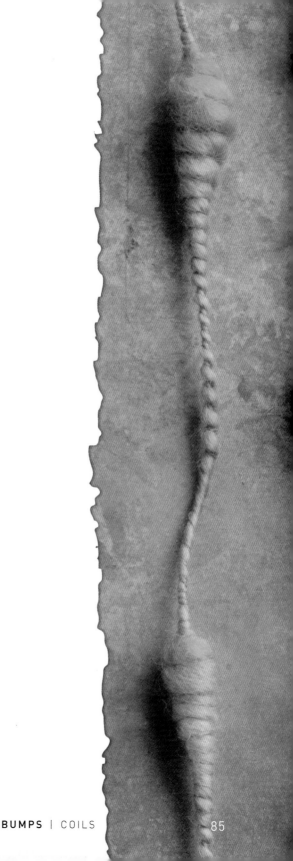

When your thick-and-thin singles is done and overspun, you can prepare your second singles yarn in one of two ways: you can spin a very thin, lightly spun singles yarn in the opposite direction from your thick-and-thin out of a fiber that doesn't have much grab to it: or, you can do something a bit quicker by grabbing a cone of strong commercial laceweight. If you go with laceweight, see the Tips section on how to introduce opposite twist into a commercially spun yarn (see page 16).

Once you have your two bobbins or your bobbin and cone, place your overspun thick-and-thin singles at your feet on the side of your back/fiber-supply hand. The laceweight goes on your front/drafting-hand side, also at your feet.

wheel setup

This technique is a tough one to grasp in the beginning because of its many steps, so for now your slowest pulley and a medium to firm uptake is best. Even with this setup, you may find yourself treadling very slowly or even pausing to let your hands catch up with your feet. Ply in the opposite direction of your thick-and-thin singles.

The sample yarn is combed Merino top for the thick and thin (Z) and commercially spun 2-ply Merino laceweight with Z-twist added. The two are then plied S.

1

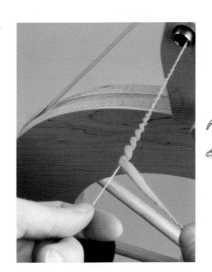

2

3

plying

Ply with even tension for a few yards. This is where all the magic happens: you're about to make a coil. Place your hands close together and close to the orifice. Keep your regular drafting hand near the plying triangle (where the two singles meet and become one yarn). Hold the laceweight straight out from the orifice and the thick-and-thin over to the side (above its own bobbin) at somewhere between a 45- and 90-degree angle. Let the thick-and-thin spiral around the laceweight. Right before you come to a thick section, pinch with the thumb and index finger on your front/drafting hand right where the two yarns meet. Roll them in the same direction that the wheel is turning, so the thinner of the yarns is wrapped at least two times around the thick-and-thin yarn (STEP 1). This is your anchor: it will keep the coil from uncoiling upward.

Now, with the laceweight still straight out from the orifice and the thick-and-thin off to the side, let the thick section wind on at that extreme angle, guiding it with your other hand in the plying triangle (STEPS 2 AND 3). Do a few treadles to take the poofiness out of the plied thick section (this only works now, before the next step) and, with the same hand, gently push the thick section up around the laceweight, leaving a short length of laceweight exposed between your two hands (STEP 4). Switch tension, and build an anchor at the bottom of the coil with the exposed laceweight by letting it wrap two times in the same spot, which will keep the coil from sliding down (STEP 5). Now spiral ply through the thin section and take a deep breath: here comes another thick section.

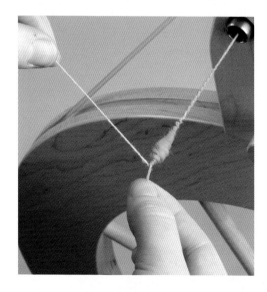

troubleshooting

Your thick-and-thin is drifting apart before you can get the thick section wound on. This happens if you let the twist from the coils you're spinning escape into the thick-and-thin between your hand and the bobbin. The easy solution to this is called your pinkie finger. When I spin a coiled yarn, my pinkie finger is busy at all times, slightly holding the singles against my hand to keep any wayward twist from wandering.

Your laceweight is getting kinked between your hand and its cone or bobbin. This is a job for your other pinkie finger. After all, one is hard at work; the other should be as well.

Your coils are too poofy and lack neat definition. After you wind on the thick section but before you push the coil up, do an extra treadle or two. This time is the only time you can affect the tightness of an individual coil. If you attempt to after you've already pushed it up, you'll be overspinning the entire yarn rather than tightening an individual coil.

Your coiled yarn is very overspun. A coiled yarn can be balanced. It's difficult for some spinners to reach this goal in the beginning because they are used to spinning rapidly. There are several steps to learn and remember. While you're learning, give yourself permission to start and stop, or at least slow down, which will make the steps easer to handle and give your yarn a better chance of being balanced. You can always use a slower whorl or overspin your thick-and-thin singles a bit more. Also check to make sure you keep your hands close together and close to the orifice. Experiment until you find the perfect combination that results in a balanced coiled yarn.

loops

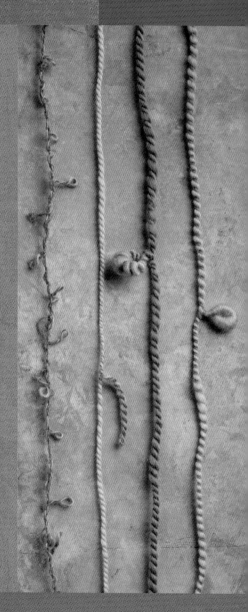

There is something magical, something bewitching, about taking yarn, which is generally thought of as linear and straight, and spinning loops into it.

These techniques are accomplished in the plying stage, but each requires a specially spun single to get the job done right. The first three techniques are wide open regarding fiber and fiber preparation choice, while the last two will work with any fiber but never as well as they work with the long and lustrous.

In this chapter, you'll discover the secrets to loading your bobbin with no fewer than five loopy wonders: the twist, a feature once regarded as little more than an accident, becomes sturdy and well-built; the twist's two variations, halos and cogs, are both newer and loopier than any yarn around; and the enduring favorite, bouclé, and her faster and only slightly less sturdy sister, fauxclé, will have you spinning circles in no time.

techniques in this chapter | twists • halos • cogs • bouclé • fauxclé

twists

This lively technique sprang from those pesky eyelash-like protuberances that unintentionally darken a bobbin when overspinning meets uneven plying. These twists, however, are designed to brighten your bobbin with their whimsy, purpose, and longevity. Short and stubby, long and sleek, matching or contrasting, scattered or cluttered, these twists can be endlessly tweaked.

singles

Any fiber or prep will work for both singles, so experiment for different effects. Both singles should be spun in the same direction so that they can be plied opposite. One ply can be commercial yarn, but take a moment to read the Tips section about introducing opposite twist to commercial yarn for better balance.

This technique relies on twist accumulation, so to get good twists you need to purposely spin one of your singles with slightly thinner sections. The thinner sections will naturally amass more twist than the surrounding yarn, so when you ply them, those sections will make sturdy, tight twists instead of fragile, poofy loops. How long your thin sections are and how often you spin them determines the final look of your yarn.

When I teach this technique to a class, I ask the participants to spin their first twist yarn with the twists in a contrasting color. This is done by spinning 2- or 3-inch sections of contrasting fiber as often as you want twists in your yarn. This helps in several ways: it encourages you to make design decisions (how often, how long); it reminds you to spin more thinly in those spots; it gives a pronounced visual cue when you go to ply; and it may just enhance your joining skills.

Whether you decide to use contrasting fiber or not, spin your singles yarn with thinner sections that are twice as long as you want your finished twists to be.

If you are going to do an even ply, place both singles yarns at your feet on your back/drafting-hand side. If you will be spiral plying, put the singles yarn you will be making the twists out of on your back/fiber-supply hand side and your other singles yarn on your front/drafting side.

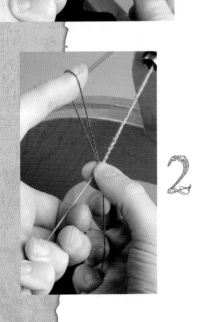

wheel setup

This technique is mostly a basic plying method, so the singles yarn you have already spun will dictate your wheel setup. Set your tension medium to high and ply in the opposite direction of your singles yarn twist.

The sample yarn is plied (S) from two handspun gray Merino and silk singles (spun Z). The twists are purple and pink silk made from 3-inch thinner sections, yielding 1½-inch twists.

plying

Join the two singles yarns to your leader and start plying. When you come to a thinner section, before it plies with the other yarn, slow your treadling down a bit and use the thumb on your front/drafting hand (the one holding the singles without the thinner sections) to pop up the

thinner section in the other ply. Specifically, bring your thumb under the thin section, about in the middle, and pop it up (STEP 1). Now, with your back/fiber-supply thumb and index finger, pinch the two ends of the thin section together and let the sides of it ply together (STEP 2). There's your twist. Be careful: if you just continue to ply, the twist isn't anchored and will likely scoot around and negatively affect the aesthetics and balance of the ply around it. So wrap the singles yarn you're holding with your front/fiber-supply hand once, counterclockwise, around the base of the twist (STEPS 3 AND 4). That wrap is enough to anchor the twist but not enough to be noticeable or affect the overall yarn. Now continue plying until you encounter another thin spot. Pop, wrap, and continue. If you find, after you have anchored each twist, that you've overplied the yarn directly in front of it, slow or stop your treadling and let the unplied yarn ply until it balances.

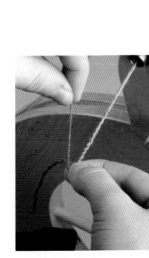

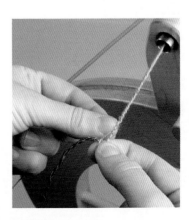

SPIN ART

halos

Perfect circles in a yarn aren't as hard to come by as you might think. Because of the perpendicular arrangement of fibers in a cocoon, when popped up and wrapped like twists, these oblong little bundles do not ply on themselves, but rather they form angelic circles.

TIPS FOR TECHNIQUE: introduce twist into commercially spun yarn for better balance (see page 16); cocoons (see page 39); twists (see page 92).

singles

Any fiber or prep will work for both singles, but one singles yarn should have some well-spun cocoons peppering its length. For cocoons destined to become halos, the tapering at the ends is less important than making the cocoon firm. Both singles yarns should be spun in the same direction.

wheel setup

This is mostly a basic plying technique, so the singles yarn you have already spun will dictate your wheel setup. Set the tension medium to high and ply in the opposite direction of the singles' twist.

The sample yarn is plied (S) from two handspun gray Merino silk singles (spun Z). The halos are gray Bluefaced Leicester.

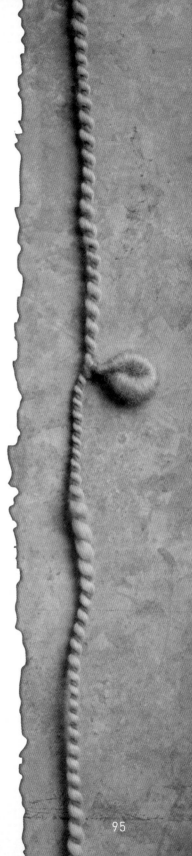

plying

Ply evenly until you come to a cocoon (STEP 1). Before the cocoon plies with the other yarn, slow your treadling down a bit and use the thumb on your front/drafting hand to pop up the cocoon in the other ply. Specifically, bring your thumb under the cocoon, about in the middle, and pop it up. Now, with your back/fiber-supply thumb and index finger, pinch the two ends of the cocoon section together and let it form a halo. To anchor, wrap the singles yarn you are holding with your front/fiber-supply hand once, counterclockwise, around the base of the halo (STEP 2). Experiment with the shape and size of your cocoons for different effects.

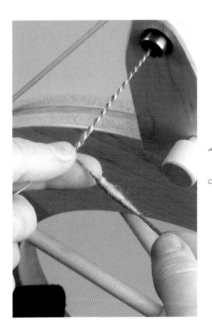

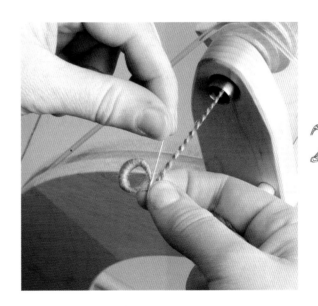

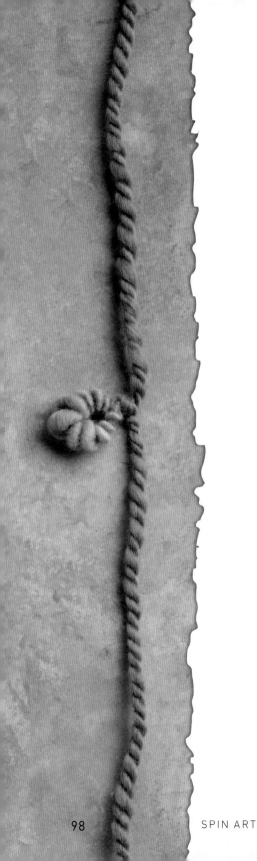

cogs

Like halos, cogs use the same hand mechanics as twists. But because of the beehives in the singles yarn, the resulting texture resembles a small cogged circle.

TIPS FOR TECHNIQUE: introduce twist into commercially spun yarn for better balance (see page 16); beehives (see page 56); twists (see page 92).

singles

Any fiber or prep will work for both singles, but one singles yarn should be loaded with beehives. Both singles should be spun in the same direction.

wheel setup

This is mostly a basic plying technique, so the singles yarn you have already spun will dictate your wheel setup. Set the tension medium to high and ply in the opposite direction of the singles' twist.

The sample yarn is plied (S) from two handspun gray Merino and silk singles (spun Z). The cogs are gray Bluefaced Leicester.

plying

Ply evenly until you come to a beehive. Before the beehive plies with the other yarn, slow your treadling down a bit and use the thumb on your front/drafting hand to pop up the beehive in the other ply. Specifically, bring your thumb under the beehive, about in the middle, and pop it up (STEP 1). Now, with your back/fiber-supply thumb

and index finger, pinch the two ends of your beehive together and let it form a cogged circle (STEP 2). To anchor, wrap the singles yarn you are holding with your front/fiber-supply hand once, counterclockwise, around the base of the cog. Now ply evenly until you come to the next beehive.

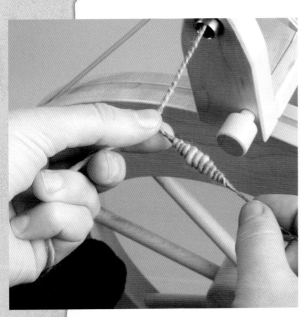

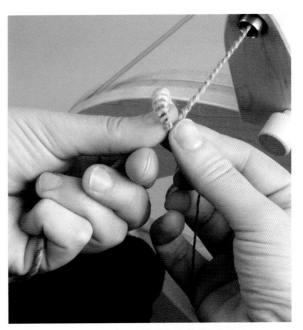

bouclé

Bouclé is French for "buckled." That's what makes this technique stand apart from all others: it buckles the yarn back on itself, creating small loops or circles. It is time consuming and includes spinning as many as three singles and plying twice. But the worthwhile end result is a stable, highly textured yarn that can be light, airy, and bulky all at the same time.

singles

A bouclé's construction relies on three plies: one to serve as a core, one to loop and buckle around the core, and one to lock the loops in place. Traditionally done with fibers such as mohair, the technique is a great use for those lustrous, long-staple fibers that draw us in with their beauty but whose utility often eludes us.

Some spinners hold that the core should be spun S and the wrap spun Z. Others say the opposite. Both are correct. Both result in a buckled yarn, though they may have slightly different final looks or feels. Judith MacKenzie McCuin gives a simple and highly adjustable instruction in *The Intentional Spinner* (Interweave, 2009): "One yarn spun left, one yarn spun right; one yarn thick, one yarn thin; one yarn low twist, one yarn high twist." Combine that approach with the correct hand mechanics, and you're bound to spin circles.

Situate yourself so that the core comes up from your front/drafting hand, and the ply that wraps around the core to make the loops rises from your back/fiber-supply hand.

wheel setup

The singles you spun for this yarn will dictate which pulley you use. But you can ply this yarn fairly fast, so do not avoid your smaller pulleys. Start with medium tension and decrease if it is pulling the yarn out of your hand before you get your circles pushed up. Ply in the opposite direction of your wrapping yarn.

The sample yarn is a thick, low-twist singles yarn of Merino wool (S) as a core with a high-twist wrapping single of mohair top (Z), plied (S) so that the mohair loosens up, making it easier to create loops, while the core tightens to become strong and stable. A thin silk thread binds the loops by being plied in the Z direction.

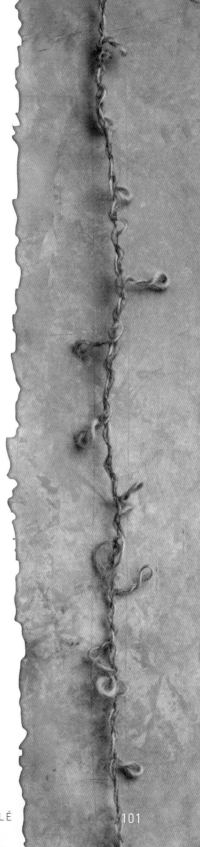

plying

Set the binder thread aside for now and join the two singles yarns to the leader. Do not expect to ply straight and even; the next step is instrumental in creating the bouclé's distinct tiny circles. Hold the core straight out from the orifice while holding the wrap out to the side, somewhere between 45 and 90 degrees and with less tension. To ensure accentuated, defined circles, don't just lay it on at this angle. Slide your fiber-supply hand back 1 inch or so (STEP 1) and quickly move that small section of wrap toward the core (STEP 2). Then, with that same hand, push the wrapped yarn slightly toward the orifice so that it creates a perfect circle around the core (STEP 3). Now slide your hand back out 1 inch or 2, move it toward the core and push it up, again and again, until either your bobbin is full or you are out of fiber. This plying takes practice, so give it time.

If you are having trouble getting circles or you find you're getting more twists than circles, don't despair because this is a common issue. Often, the problem is that the push toward the orifice is too slow or too far. If you let the two singles yarns ply too much before you push up, the wrapping yarn will be too tight to loop for you. Conversely, if you push it up fast but too far, you get plied twists instead of loops. Try to slow your treadling down and push the wrapping yarn up slowly. You should see the moment that the circles start to form. Try to maintain this motion as you speed back up.

SPIN ART

At this point, you should have a bobbin full of fun circles. Sadly, they are sliding around on an unbalanced core. The following step addresses both of these issues by plying the yarn in the opposite, balancing direction with a binder that locks the circles and loops into place. Place your buckled 2-ply at your feet on your back/fiber-supply hand side and the locking thread at your feet on your front/drafting-hand side. Do this second ply in the opposite direction of the previous ply, which should bring the entire yarn to balance.

The sample yarn is plied with the binder in a clockwise (Z) direction.

Ply the buckled 2-ply and locking thread together, holding the locking thread straight out from the orifice and the buckled yarn at a slight angle. Let the buckled yarn wrap around the locking thread (STEP 4). If you use uneven tension for this step, make sure your binding thread has enough tensile strength because you don't want it to break now or later when you are working with the yarn. But you do not have to ply these with uneven tension. Experiment to see which tension gives you the look you want with the materials you have chosen. Stop and check your yarn. Is it balanced? Does it need more twist? Less twist? If you achieve the right amount of ply twist, you will see those loops really bloom. With too much or too little, they can look a bit squat.

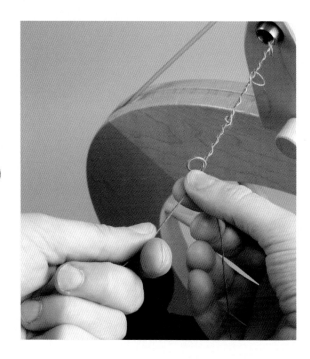

SPIN ART

fauxclé

I believe in respecting and learning as much as possible about this craft that I love, but that doesn't mean that I don't occasionally give into the inclination to be lazy. This technique was born of that laziness. When I wanted to create a bouclé-like yarn without having to spin two or three singles and ply twice, I decided to combine the anchoring system I created for some other techniques with a shorthand version of the buckled classic. The result is a yarn that looks and acts like a bouclé, but requires only half the work.

TIPS FOR TECHNIQUE: introduce twist into commercially spun yarn for better balance (see page 16); bouclé (see page 101).

singles

The technique requires one high-twist singles yarn, preferably in long wool or mohair, which will be the wrapping ply, and another singles yarn or commercially spun laceweight that will act as the core. If you spin the core by hand, go thin, smooth, and with low twist and spin it in the opposite direction of the wrapping singles. If you use commercially spun laceweight, be sure to read the Tips section in this book and introduce some twist opposite to what you will be plying.

wheel setup

Set your wheel on a medium to fast pulley and make sure your uptake is a little less than medium. You want it to pull in the yarn when you release it but not pull the yarn from your hands. Ply in the opposite direction of your wrapping single.

The sample yarn is a yearling mohair singles yarn (Z) wrapped (S) around a core of 2-ply commercial laceweight with Z-twist introduced.

plying

The mechanics of plying for this technique are generally the same as for bouclé except for the addition of anchors, which you will insert every 2 inches or so. So, follow the instructions and pictures for the bouclé technique, but after every two or three push-ups, switch tension by pulling the wrapping ply straight from the orifice and the core ply out to the side at a 90-degree angle. Let it wrap a few times in the same spot

(STEP 1). This creates an anchor that the loops in the preceding few inches will not slide past. The idea is not to anchor every loop, but to insert an anchor every few inches, so although the loops may slide around a bit, they don't go far.

If you find when you switch tension to create your anchor that your last circle gets pulled out by your wheel's uptake, decrease the tension a bit. If this

does not work for you, build in an extra loop, knowing that the tension might pull it out.

Don't feel like you need to fill every bit of space in your yarn with loops. One loop per knitted stitch fills out the fabric nicely, so depending on the thickness of your yarn, you might only need a circle every inch or so. Now, with all the time you've saved, you could spin another yarn.

1

multi-plies

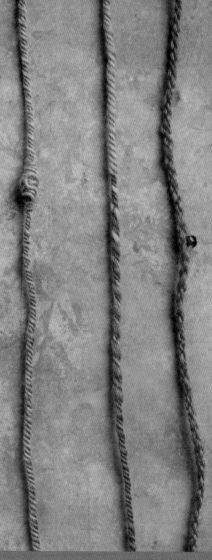

There comes a time when every spinner needs to break out of the singles slump and 2-ply trough—when he or she has to "spinner up" and create something that takes more time but also lasts longer.

More plies will make a yarn rounder and even out thin or thick spots that exist in any of the individual singles. They also increase a yarn's durability: three, four, or five plies are much harder to abrade than one or two. Multi-plied yarns may take more time, but they will also last longer and look better for doing it.

This chapter focuses on four spinning techniques that feature three or more plies: Chain plying is famous for maintaining fabulous color sections and infamous for rousing spinners into debate. Chain stacks retain these same color sections, but matching stacks add stripy 3-ply texture. Cabling makes a wonderful, rugged, round yarn, and with cabled foreign objects, you will attach small things to your yarn far more firmly than ever before. Let's ply away!

techniques in this chapter | chain plying • chain stacks • cables • cabled foreign objects

chain plying

Many spinners find themselves confounded about how to translate handpainted fiber's beauty into yarn form. Chain plying is much loved for doing that very thing. It is a 3-plylike yarn spun from a singles yarn so that color separations and changes along the length are maintained. This is not a true 3-ply, but a singles yarn being chained onto itself, and as such is theoretically not as sturdy as a true 3-ply. But I've never had one give out on me. Because of its method of construction, a small bump is created each time the chain is looped. Some spinners find these bumps troublesome, others do not. Still, even with these issues, it creates a lovely stripy yarn. This technique is sometimes known incorrectly as "Navajo plying," but this term is slowly being replaced by the more aptly descriptive "chain plying."

singles

Any singles will work, and you only need one. Chain plying is used to its full potential when the singles is spun out of a multicolor fiber with long color changes. Chain-plied yarns are easy to overply, so build some extra twist into your singles (it should have a bit more twist than if it were going to make a standard 2- or 3-ply yarn), and you will be less likely to have this problem. Also, you will need to spin three times the length you want your final yarn to be, since you will be creating a 3-ply yarn out of one singles. Since this is just one singles yarn and not three, take special care to not spin any thin or weak spots in it; if one spot wears out in this yarn, you do not have two other plies staying strong. You will also find it beneficial to let your singles sit for a day or two, just to relax any kinks, which will make the plying easier.

wheel setup

Since this yarn is easy to overply, start with your wheel set one pulley bigger than if you were going to ply your singles traditionally. Select a strong uptake.

The sample yarn is Polwarth wool top handpainted with extremely long color changes, though I stripped them shorter so that the effect could be seen in the small swatch. It is spun Z and chain-plied S.

plying

Put your singles on a lazy kate and attach it to a fresh bobbin's leader. Using the singles, make a loop. Hold the loop open and close to your body with a few fingers on your front/drafting hand, while your back/fiber-supply hand holds the singles yarn leading to the bobbin (STEP 1). Your front/drafting hand, the one that holds the loop, should remain close to your body the entire time you are spinning this yarn. You will use your back/fiber-supply hand to carry the singles back and forth from your body to the orifice.

Start treadling in the opposite direction of your singles twist. Bring the singles close to the loop and reach through the loop with the index

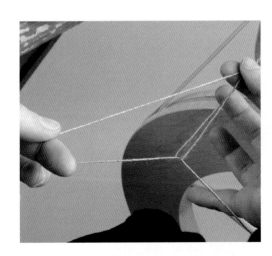

finger of your front/drafting hand (the one holding the loop open) **(STEP 2)**. Your back/fiber-supply hand is now pinching the three strands above the loop **(STEP 3)**. Move that hand evenly toward the orifice, keeping your front/drafting hand close to your body. This will, at once, feed the previously chained yarn into the orifice and pull new singles off the lazy-kated bobbin. You will now have a large loop stretching from your body to the orifice. Slowly slide your back/fiber-supply hand down the singles toward your body, creating a chain-plied yarn **(STEP 4)**.

Slide your fingers down to your front/drafting hand so that it

creates a small loop you can reach through with your front/drafting index finger **(STEP 5)**. This creates a new loop. Your back/fiber-supply hand should pinch above the loop and once again move the yarn toward the orifice and back again toward you.

Once you are accustomed to the mechanics of chain plying, notice the following: as you slide your back/fiber-supply hand toward your body along the yarn's length, you will feel (and see) where the singles loops onto itself at the point where you ply past the chain intersection. Many spinners find this "bump" bothersome. With some fibers,

it may help to give this spot a little roll with your fingers as you pass. Also, when your back/fiber-supply hand is traveling toward your body, be careful to use even tension to ply all three strands evenly so that you are not letting the third strand wrap around the other two.

Chain plying can be tricky to figure out and may take a while to get comfortable with, but once you do, it can be a meditative plying technique that will give you perfect stripes every time. In fact, there is no reason you can't chain ply nontraditional singles: try it with thick-and-thin or textured singles.

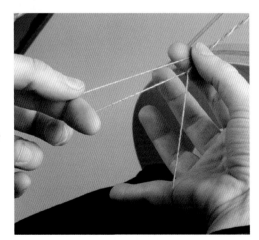

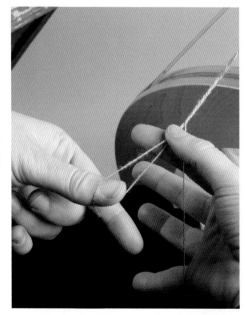

chain stacks

Just because you are set on maintaining gorgeous color sequencing does not mean you can't introduce a little extra texture to your yarn. This technique combines chain plying and stacks for stripy, bumpy goodness.

TIPS FOR TECHNIQUE: chain plying (see page 110); stacks (see page 75).

singles

Prepare a singles yarn with some extra twist, just like for chain plying. Again, striped fiber shows this technique to its fullest, and letting your singles rest for a few days will make it a bit easier to work with.

wheel setup

Since this yarn is easy to overply, start with your wheel set one pulley bigger than if you were going to ply your singles yarn traditionally. Select a strong uptake.

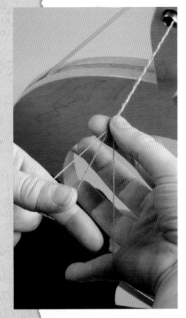

plying

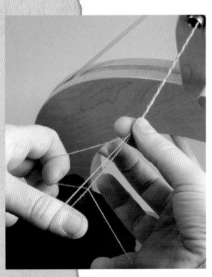

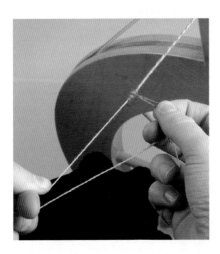

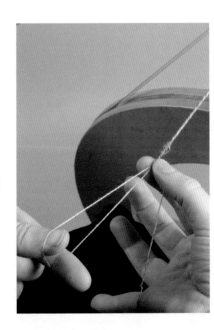

As with chain plying, create a loop (STEP 1), reach through the loop (STEP 2), and move your back/fiber-supply hand toward the orifice. Now, though, instead of moving slowly back toward your body and creating an even chain-plied 3-ply, this is where you are going to create a stack. You should have a loop stretching from your body to where the chain loops onto itself several inches from the orifice (where your back/fiber-supply hand is pinching). Your back/fiber-supply hand is holding one strand in front of that chain loop and doubled strand that makes up the loop coming from the lazy-kated bobbin. It is time to build the stack. Let the doubled strand that makes the loop coming from the lazy kate wrap on at a 90-degree angle (STEP 3) until your stack meets the bump where the chain loops onto itself (STEP 4). Now, switch back to even tension and evenly slide your hand down the length, creating a 3-chain-plied yarn.

Each time you chain loop, you can create a chain stack. The shorter the loops you create, the closer your chain stacks will be, and the longer your loops, the farther apart they will be. Knowing this makes it very easy to evenly distribute stacks throughout your yarn or to place them sporadically.

cables

One of the hardest working yarns in a spinner's repertoire is the cable. Its rugged round beauty is like a siren song to the seasoned spinner. If you want a yarn that will last forever and make stitch patterns pop, this is it. Once you spin a few cables, spice things up by combining that with other textural techniques. You can cable coils, supercoils, stacks, thick-and-thin, and many more. I should briefly mention here that when you ply already-plied yarns together, it is called "cabling." It cuts down on confusion to refrain from calling it plying.

singles

Any fiber or fiber prep will work, but the key to making lovely cables is understanding that the feel and look of the finished yarn depends most heavily on the singles you initially spin. If they have too much twist, your cables will turn out heavy and ropelike. Spin your four singles loose and with little twist, and your finished yarn will bloom. The singles can be spun in either direction, but all should be the same.

wheel setup

For the singles yarn, set your wheel on a medium to large pulley (depending on your yarn weight) with a firm uptake. This will give you a loose singles. For the first round of plying, use a smaller pulley with a medium uptake (this will overply). For the final round of plying, you will want a slightly bigger pulley (but not as big as for the singles) with a firm uptake.

The sample yarn is spun from Merino wool, two pink and two gray singles spun Z, each plied with the other color (plied S), and the resulting plied yarns cabled together (cabled Z).

plying

First, loosely spin two sets of two (four altogether) singles. Next, create two 2-ply yarns by plying two of the singles together in the opposite direction than they were spun. Be sure to overply these yarns quite a bit. At this point, you should have two bobbins of 2-ply yarn (STEP 1). Finally, balance these overplied 2-plies by cabling them together (plying in the opposite direction of their ply) (STEP 2). For example, if you spin your singles with a Z twist (like I did), you'll overply in the S direction to yield two bobbins of 2-ply, and finally cable in the Z direction, creating a balanced, cabled 4-ply yarn.

1

2

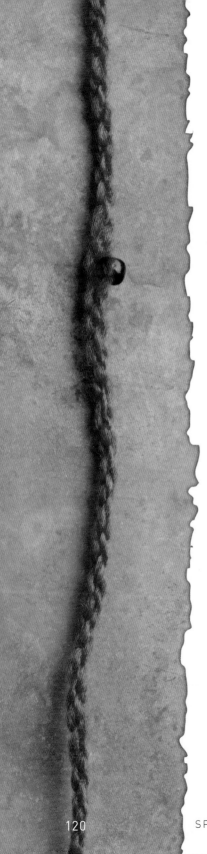

cabled foreign objects

Finally, you can have your cables and foreign objects, too. This yarn has all the structure and durability of a cable, with the whimsy and texture of small foreign objects.

TIPS FOR TECHNIQUE: stringing foreign objects (see page 62; variation: strung and plied (see page 64)); cables (see page 117).

singles

Just like for standard cables, any fiber or fiber prep will work, and the singles should be lightly spun. But before you start to ply, use a needle and string one (or more) of your singles with whatever small, light foreign object you choose.

wheel setup

For the singles, set your wheel on a medium to large pulley (depending on your yarn weight) with a firm uptake. This will give you a loose singles yarn. For the first round of plying, use a smaller pulley with a medium uptake (this will overply). For the final round of plying, you will want a slightly bigger pulley (but not as big as for the singles) with a firm uptake.

The sample yarn is spun from a Bluefaced Leicester and silk mix spun Z, one singles yarn loaded with small seed beads then plied S, and the resulting plied yarns cabled together in the Z direction.

plying

During the plying process (don't forget to add extra ply twist), whenever it strikes your fancy, grab one of the foreign objects and ply past it. You should now have two 2-ply yarns, one or both loaded with foreign objects (STEP 1). Now cable the two together and the foreign objects will be held firmly in place (STEP 2).

1

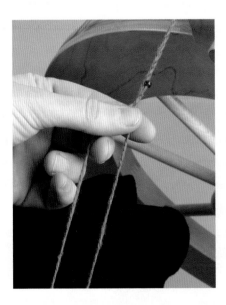

2

combinations

Yarns can move from predictable to remarkable when you create them by using combined techniques. Some possible combinations involve developing added dexterity or changing the look of the yarn to such a degree that it is valid to call them techniques in their own right.

Each of the four techniques you will find in this chapter start with basic corespinning and grow bigger and bolder from there. It will serve you and your yarn well if you take a few minutes to review corespinning, Chapter 2.

While this chapter is by no means an exhaustive list of textured combinations, you will find that "bubblewrapping" contradicts my very own advice, "corehive" demonstrates that a teacher is always learning, "Rip Torn" takes a fun technique and increases its knitability, and "Tex Ritter" challenges you to spin a layered singles yarn. All four textured combinations keep your mind and fingers on the ball as they stun and stagger your eyes.

techniques in this chapter | bubblewrapping • corehive • rip torn • tex ritter

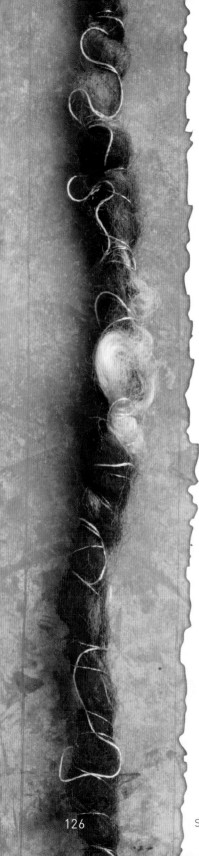

bubblewrapping

Bubblewrapping grows from the question, "What happens if you ply a corespun yarn?" I mention in Chapter 2 that corespun yarns are not usually plied, lest the wrapping fiber come unwrapped and pool around the core in a shapeless, feeble mass. Bubblewrapping is an exception, named so for how the final look reminds me of the plastic packing bubbles that my children love to pop, pop, pop.

TIPS FOR TECHNIQUE: corespinning (see page 32); autowrap (see page 25); spiral plying (see page 72).

singles

You will need a bobbin of autowrapped corespun yarn with a 2-ply core with no opposite twist added (this core will have started out balanced but will now, after corespinning, have active twist in one direction or the other). You will also need another strand—a commercially spun or handspun singles (spun in the same direction as the autowrapped corespun yarn) will work. Since the strength of the final yarn will not rest on this second strand, some threads will work, but I would still stay away from weak thread.

Place the corespun yarn at your feet on your front/drafting-hand side, and the other strand at your feet on the other side. If you are using a spool of thread (like I am), place it in a small bowl so you don't have to chase it across the floor.

wheel setup

Set up your wheel slightly faster (one pulley smaller) than how you set it to spin the corespun yarn but with less tension. Ply in the opposite direction of your corespun yarn.

The sample yarn was corespun clockwise with an autowrap of green thread and is plied counterclockwise (S) with a sturdy strand of metallic gold.

plying

Attach the autowrapped corespun yarn to the leader along with the other strand. Hold the corespun yarn straight out from the orifice and, with a firm hand, the other strand out at an angle somewhere between 70 and 90 degrees (STEP 1). As you start to ply, let the other strand wrap around the corespun yarn much in the way an autowrap wraps. Because you are holding it firmly, it will bundle down more tightly than the autowrap. Before you release the yarn into the orifice, let enough twist accumulate so that the fibers are almost straight again and begin to bubble up between the original autowrap and this wrapping strand (STEP 2). At this point, the core should be back to its original balanced state.

Now just for a minute, imagine plying a corespun yarn without the two wraps. Can you see why I recommend against it? The words "shapeless, feeble mass" come to mind. Bubblewrapping may not create the sturdiest of yarns, but the two wraps help minimize the abrasion that the fibers receive, and when you are done, you get a big, poofy, unique yarn that is warmer than most and weighs almost nothing.

1

2

corehive

A while back, I taught a spinner how to corespin and beehive. She had the inventive idea of putting the two together. Not only did she combine them, she did so by corespinning a batt of sky blues and forming the beehives out of stark white Merino so that they exploded out like big puffy clouds. The yarn was gorgeous, and prompted me to study, and subsequently start teaching, corehive—or beecore, if you like.

TIPS FOR TECHNIQUE: corespun (see page 32); beehives (see page 56), introduce twist into commercially spun yarn for better balance (see page 16).

fiber

Take a few minutes to read in Chapters 2 and 3 (respectively) about the fibers needed for corespinning and beehives. Corehive is a corespun yarn, so you need a core (see the Tips section if you are using a commercial yarn as a core) and some wrapping fiber. Corehive also contains beehives, so prepare as many beehive fiber bundles as you want in the yarn.

Place the core at your feet on your front/drafting-hand side and the beehive bundles within reach.

wheel setup

If there is anything slower than a beehive yarn, it is a corespun beehive yarn. Use your biggest pulley and very little tension as a starting point. This yarn can be spun in either direction but should be spun with balancing the core in mind.

The sample yarn has a commercially spun 2-ply core with Z twist added, wrapped with carded fiber corespun counterclockwise with Merino and silk beehives.

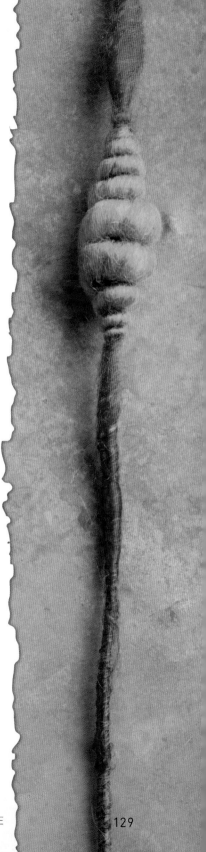

spinning

Corespin for a while without adding beehives because, as with any heavily textured yarn, including textural features too early in the yarn can sometimes make casting on or binding off (when knitting) more difficult. When you are ready to add a beehive, grab a prepared bundle and place one end on top of the unwrapped core. Corespin over the tapered end of the beehive to anchor it (STEP 1), then predraft the corespinning fiber so that it is fairly thin. Now, move the corespinning fiber into the same hand that holds the core, treating both as if they are a singles yarn, and build the beehive with your back/fiber-supply hand (STEP 2). Once the beehive is built (STEP 3) and pushed up (STEP 4), and all that remains is the tapered tip, move the corespinning fiber back into your back/fiber-supply hand, hold the tapered end of the beehive against the core, and corespin over it to give the bottom an anchor (STEP 5). Continue corespinning until the next spot screams out for a beehive.

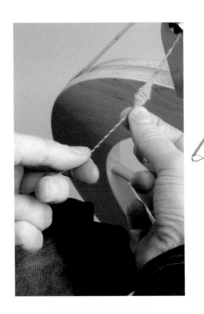

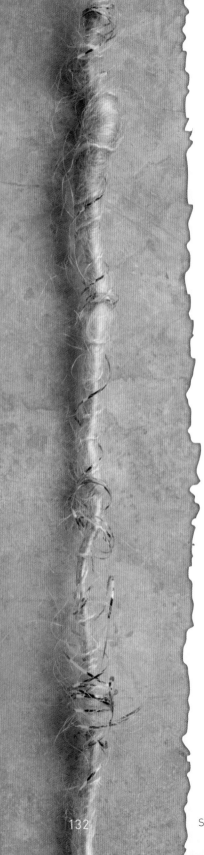

rip torn

I used to call this technique "in-and-out tornado," which in a hurry I would shorten to "i'n' o torn." This eventually morphed into the moniker of the award-winning actor. The combination itself emerged from my love of the tornado and corespinning techniques and my desire to combine them for style and functionality.

TIPS FOR TECHNIQUE: introduce twist into commercially spun yarn for better balance (see page 16); tornados (see page 28); corespinning (see page 32); racing stripe (see page 22); autowrap (see page 25).

fiber

This technique requires the supplies for both a corespun yarn (a core and carded fiber) and a tornado yarn (extra wrapping strands or threads).

Place the core at your feet on one side and the tornado strands on the other.

wheel setup

We are combining a slow technique with a technique that requires very little twist, so the wheel setup here is slow, slow, slow. Pick a large pulley and a medium-to-firm uptake. Rip Torn only goes through the wheel once, and depending on how you prepare the core, it can be spun in either direction.

The sample yarn features a textured batt wrapped around a commercially spun 2-ply laceweight (with S-twist added) and a tornado of brushed mohair, a silk thread, a metallic thread, and a simple cotton thread. The yarn is spun Z.

spinning

Attach all the strands to the leader and start spinning, letting them all racing stripe around the singles. After a few inches, start corespinning, using all the strands as a core (STEP 1). When you are ready to bring the tornado out, predraft the fiber so that it is thin for a couple of inches, or for as long as you want the tornado to be visible. Now switch hands, taking all the strands except the core in your back/fiber-supply hand and holding the predrafted section along with the core in your front hand (STEP 2). Start making a tornado using the required shuffling motion (see Chapter 1) (STEP 3). The tornado can be super short so that it pokes out for just a knitted stitch or two, or it can be long enough to knit a stripe, but when you

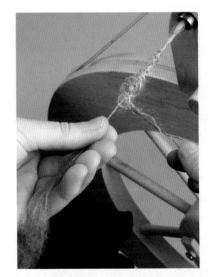

are ready to tuck the tornado back in, simply switch hands again, moving all the strands back to your drafting hand with the core, and returning the carded fiber to your back/supply hand (STEP 4). Resume corespinning until you want to whip up another tornado.

You don't have to use all the tornado strands each time. You can make different tornados, depending on which strands you leave in and which you take out. You can even have sections where you intersperse tornadoes and simple corespinning into a length of racing stripe or autowrap (STEP 5). The options are numerous, and the resulting yarn will be unique.

tex ritter

One of my son's favorite songs was Tex Ritter's version of "The Wayward Wind": he even sang it for a drama class audition when he was about four years old. When the technique I referred to as "textured rope" got shortened to "tex rope," the minor leap to Tex Ritter seemed altogether natural. So that's what this technique is called, but it's more like textured rope than a deep-voiced country crooner. It yields a dramatic yarn that gives your brain and fingers a workout as they labor to construct all three layers. It can be thick and dense or light and airy, but it's always an eye-catcher.

TIPS FOR TECHNIQUE: autowrap (see page 25); corespinning (see page 32).

fiber

This yarn is a three-layer yarn, and each layer is a different material. The first layer is a mishmash of fiber, carded batts, locks, scraps, felted bits and baubles, and anything else you might find drifting around your work space. The second layer is loose, fluffy mohair. The mohair should be in cloud form. If it is in lock form or combed, pull it out and fluff it by hand or card it. The third layer is a prespun singles yarn that can be handspun or commercially spun.

Arrange the first layer of loose fiber in your lap, your mohair cloud within grabbing range, and the wrapping yarn at your feet on your front/drafting-hand side, directly below the orifice.

wheel setup

A Tex Ritter yarn is bulky and will only go through the wheel once, so it does not need much twist. Choose the biggest pulley and set your tension somewhere between medium and firm.

The sample yarn is Z spun and boasts a first layer of locks, batts, and scraps, a second layer of yellow mohair clouds, and an outer layer of gold commercial yarn.

spinning

This technique can be challenging at first, but once you get the hang of it, you will be Tex Rittering along to a steady beat. It is easiest, when learning, to add the layers slowly.

Layer 1, Singles The first layer is a singles out of the fiber in your lap, so grab a bit of it with your back/fiber-supply hand and start spinning by drafting it out just enough to make a yarn, letting lumps and bumps form as they may (STEP 1). This is going to be bulky, so make sure your feet are slow moving.

Layer 2, Mohair Cloud Keep spinning the textured singles, but at the same time, grab a small amount of teased mohair. With your back/fiber-supply hand, reach in front of your front/drafting hand and corespin the already-formed singles with the mohair (STEP 2). In this case, the mohair is the wrap and the bumpy singles is the core. Wrap it until your two hands meet and

1

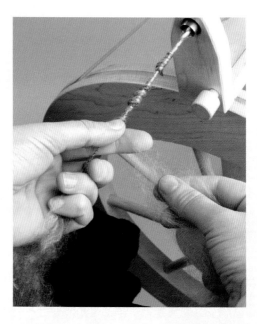

2

only then let the wrapped yarn feed into the orifice. Now, grab more fiber from your lap, spin some more textured singles (STEP 3), then wrap it with the mohair.

Layer 3, Autowrapping When you are handling the first two layers with relative ease, the third layer should be a breeze.

Grab the prespun yarn and place it at your feet, directly below the orifice, so there is as little tension on it as possible. Attach the prespun yarn to the yarn (usually you will do this at the beginning by attaching it to your leader, but for attaching it in the middle of a yarn, let it act as the core of your singles for a few inches), then drop it and let it

autowrap around the other two layers (STEP 4). Make sure that it is wrapping around the yarn after you wrap the singles with mohair: it should be the third or top layer. It should not only show prominently but also serves to bundle the mohair layer a bit. That's it. Both hands work hard, three layers get built.

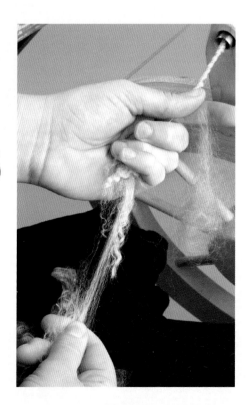

afterword

This book was born of my desire to spin fantastic yarns, as well as gather existing knowledge about spinning textured yarns, add to it, and improve it where possible, so that I could form a method for making structurally sound, balanced yarns that are texturally daring. I hope this book can find a home in the spinning canon, and that you or the spinner sitting next to you improves and adds to it further, so that we all learn and grow. To that end, I encourage every spinner to keep learning. Read and learn everything you can about spinning (or whatever craft you feel passionate about). There are many wonderful teachers and spinners out there, so take classes and workshops. Join a guild. Spin with friends. The more you learn, the more you'll know what fiber can and can't do, how it will act in different situations, and how to use it to create the yarns you envision. Learning more will make you a better all-around spinner. It continues to do that for me.

All the techniques in this book are products of experimentation, by me and generations before me. In your creative endeavors, try to put aside any stubbornness or fear and just keep experimenting. Don't be afraid to try new things, to fail, to create ugly yarns, to overspin, to undertwist. The worst thing you'll do is waste a bit of time and fiber, and the best is that you will create something you love. Either way, you'll learn something.

Spinning and knitting have vastly changed my life. I get to make my living doing something that makes my heart and my head happy. I get to produce beautiful, useful yarn and knitted objects. More amazing, and something I wouldn't trade for all the guanaco fiber in the world, is the community and friends that I've gained through this craft. They have made my life richer and warmer. I can't say this enough: if you love to make yarn or use yarn, there are people out there just like you, with things to learn from you and to teach to you. Whatever you do, just keep spinning!

index

Be inspired by yarn

Explore these expert spinning resources from Interweave

Get Spun
The Step-by-Step Guide to
Spinning Art Yarns
Symeon North
ISBN 978-1-59668-064-7
$22.95

Start Spinning
Everything You Need to
Know to Make Great Yarn
Maggie Casey
ISBN 978-1-59668-065-4
$21.95

The Intentional Spinner
with DVD
A Holistic Approach
to Making Yarn
Judith MacKenzie McCuin
ISBN 978-1-59668-360-0
$29.95